# Dilemmas in Teaching:

## Cases for Collaborative Faculty Reflection

CENTER FOR TEACHING EXCELLENCE
Canisius College

# Dilemmas in Teaching:
## Cases for Collaborative Faculty Reflection

*Edited by:*
*Chris M. Anson*
*Lesley K. Cafarelli*
*Carol Rutz*
*Michelle R. Weis*

*The Collaboration for the Advancement of*
*College Teaching & Learning*
MENDOTA PRESS
AN IMPRINT OF MAGNA PUBLICATIONS, INC.
Madison, Wisconsin

Printed in the United States of America

ISBN 0-912150-51-3

5  4  3  2  1

Mendota Press, an imprint of Magna Publications
2718 Dryden Drive
Madison, Wisconsin 53704
Fax: 608-246-3597
Telephone orders: 800-433-0499

# Contents

# Case Listing with Abstracts

## Part II: Cases about Classrooms

### Case 1. Critical Thinking or Thinking Critically

*James H. Smith, Northern State University*

A political science professor tries to demonstrate his views on critical thinking by writing to the student newspaper and through specific requirements on writing assignments. Students resist his approach, both in and out of the classroom.

### Case 2. Group Cases: One Professor's Dilemma

*Srinivasan Ragothaman, University of South Dakota*

This case features a single mother, a basketball player, and a grading policy adopted by an instructor. This case addresses certain risks associated with using the case method in the classroom. Cooperative learning and grading issues are also highlighted.

### Case 3. Judgment Day

*Marie McNeff, Augsburg College*

This case involves a professor and adult learners in a weekend college introductory philosophy class who jointly decide on criteria by which the professor will be evaluated. The students then judge the professor on what seems to be a different set of criteria. The student evaluations result in reprimands by the department chair and academic dean.

### Case 4. The Loafing Letdown

*Ronald A. Klocke, Mankato State University*

A new assistant professor of management finds that student teams are plagued by varying levels of participation and commitment. The issue is complicated by surprising ratings on their peer evaluations of group work.

### Case 5. The Case of the Harassed Teacher

*Tony Filipovitch and Mary McDearmon, Mankato State University*

A woman teacher finds offensive graffiti in her classroom and tries to enlist her male co-teacher in a confrontation strategy. Issues of gender, power, and responsibility for a safe teaching environment come bubbling up as they consider the options.

### Case 6. Yes, Virginia, You're in a Pickle

*Mary R. DeMaine, College of Visual Arts*

A junior faculty member re-applying for promotion tries to put student complaints and a colleague's sabotage into perspective. The faculty member's strong teaching and service to the department were misread by a previous review panel. Consequently, she must undo the damage of the unsuccessful review to make a successful case this time.

### Case 7. Too Much Thinking

*Richard Jewell, University of Minnesota-Twin Cities*

This composite of several real-life students and teachers examines Janice, a single mother who has done well in practical courses, and Dr. Terrence, her professor in a critical writing and thinking course. Janice wants to withdraw because she finds the course too difficult. Dr. Terrence is concerned about whether Janice is capable of abstract thought and, if she is, what role he should play in helping her.

### Case 8. Grade Expectations

*Jeannine L. Saabye, University of Mary*

A professor with rigorous standards feels lonely and threatened when a dissatisfied student marshals other students to complain about the professor's grading system. Issues of standards, student preparation, teacher-student expectations, and faculty accountability all mix together in this case.

### Case 9. The Jonas Incident

*Chris M. Anson, University of Minnesota-Twin Cities*

Writing teachers are used to seeing papers develop rhetorically and stylistically as students become more practiced in the writing process. In this case, a student submits a paper that is well written according to objective criteria, even though the writer did not revise between drafts. However, the content wars with the instructor's values and makes assessment an ideological rather than a rhetorical act.

## Part III: Cases about Departments and Institutions

### Case 10. The Academic Purist

*Deborah Petersen-Perlman, University of Minnesota-Duluth*

This case features the struggle of a classically trained professor who has come to desire change in her lecture-driven classes. The professor connects with a peer observer to facilitate new directions in her teaching. She finds herself resistant to change, and most particularly to relinquishing control so as to encourage more active student participation.

### Case 11. Best in the Class

*Carol Rutz, University of Minnesota-Twin Cities*

What happens when an outstanding student participates fully in a writing class, writes exceptionally well, and claims to be dissatisfied? In this case the teacher and the student have radically different views of the course: The teacher is thrilled with the student's work; the student's course-evaluation comments may doom the teacher's future teaching assignment.

### Case 12. The Fly in the Ointment

*James Swanson, Dakota State University*

This is a case of a faculty member who invokes the protection of academic freedom to resist the changes and teaching innovations required by his institution's accreditation plan. It raises the question of how other faculty and faculty development coordinators can encourage their colleagues to be open to strengthening their teaching on the basis of new pedagogical research and theory.

### Case 13. Risky Business

*Lesley K. Cafarelli, The Collaboration for the Advancement of College Teaching & Learning*

This case is about a department chair faced with decisions about a tenure-track professor in a department rife with political tensions about the evaluation of teaching. While the junior faculty member has received positive evaluations in the past and has been involved in faculty development activities, the chair is accosted by concerns from a complaining student and an entrenched senior professor, as well as a mandate on evaluation from the university's new vice-president.

### Case 14. To 'B' or Not To 'B': A Case of Academic Appeal

*Benedict J. Arogyaswamy, University of South Dakota*

This case involves a student who feels that the professor wasted class time, leading to a poor grade for the student. Several issues crop up—cultural biases, academic freedom, and the fairness of academic appeal procedures. Sample focus questions are included.

### Case 15. To Tell or Not To Tell

*Shamsul Huda, Argiro L. Morgan, and William Serban, Xavier University of Louisiana*

While working on a collaborative project with a male colleague, a young female faculty member inadvertently learns from a student that her colleague harbors prejudice against a minority group. Confronting her colleague would violate the confidentiality of the student's disclosure as well as endanger the collaborative endeavor. Seniority, diversity, gender, and tenure criteria are some issues addressed in this case.

### Case 16. Unpopular Senior Professor

*Bruce L. Smith, University of South Dakota*

A department chair struggles to manage a department high in faculty turnover that also has a senior professor who is unpopular with students and very resistant to change. The professor says his high standards are resisted by students who prefer easier instructors. The students say the professor is rigid and more interested in preserving his image of being tough than with helping them to learn.

### Case 17. Wendy Lamb

*Tom Mason and Melissa Shepard, University of St. Thomas*

A capable junior faculty member participates in a faculty development program designed to focus on one of her physics courses. To her dismay, the students show little enthusiasm for the course, and several drop. As a result, the professor is too upset to take advantage of the mentoring opportunity offered by her faculty development partner.

### Case 18. Assessment at Woebegone State

*Lesley K. Cafarelli, The Collaboration for the Advancement of College Teaching & Learning*

A hard-working psychology professor chairs an assessment task force that attempts to please everyone: the accrediting body, the university administration, the faculty, and the members of the task force itself. The proposed assessment plan meets resistance at a number of levels, and the chair despairs of bringing people together on a solid plan.

### Case 19. Is Something Rotten in Denmark?

*Rebecca Kamm, Northeast Iowa Community College*

Two professors, one from an American college and the other one from Europe, compare notes on their experiences as exchange professors. They discover that expectations, preparation, and the collegial environment can all be improved to make such exchanges successful for the participants, their student, and their academic institution.

### Case 20. Teaching Semantics: Euphemisms, Taboos, and Obscenities

*Richard Betting, Valley State University*

This case studies the power of language—even when teachers and students study language itself in an attempt to understand how it influences us. Students who object to any encounter with taboo language enact a distressing dilemma for linguists: Naming the taboo invokes an emotional response that prevents the scholarly examination of that kind of language.

## Part IV: Cases About the Changing Culture as It Affects Higher Education

### Case 21. The Cancer Student

*Carol Rutz, University of Minnesota-Twin Cities*

A college senior asks her writing teacher for an incomplete. Risky cancer treatment is scheduled for the last three weeks of the student's final spring term. The teacher has to consider the student's needs, the institution's rules, and her own (the teacher's) sense of what is proper under the circumstances.

## Case 22.  Facing the Reality of Students' Preparation and Research Skills

*Deborah Petersen-Perlman and Marilyn Russell-Bogle, University of Minnesota-Duluth*

A communications professor and a university librarian join forces to develop a challenging assignment for a first-year mass communications course. Both are disappointed by students' perception of the assignment as too demanding; they worry that students are unprepared for college-level research—and unwilling to make up the deficit by working hard.

## Case 23.  Faltering Steps under the Americans with Disabilities Act

*Richard W. Metcalf, University of South Dakota*

This case uses a generic college course setting to highlight a series of decisions confronting an instructor with ADA requirements. The case focuses on the issues of the course syllabus, make-up examinations, and incomplete grading.

## Case 24.  Jalen

*Eugene Hermitte and Phyllis Worthy Dawkins, Johnson C. Smith University*

In this case, a white professor encounters difficulties teaching African subject matter to African-American students. An African-American professor observes the class, interviews students, and presents her reflections to the professor.

## Case 25.  Special Circumstances

*Jeannine L. Saabye, University of Mary*

Despite a professor's careful course planning and ample notification, a student has an unavoidable conflict on two important class days. The teacher and student must work together on what seems an insoluble problem.

## Case 26.  They're Acting Really Squirrely

*Thomas D. Peacock, University of Minnesota-Duluth*

In this case (designed for use in secondary education teacher-training programs), Dale, a school principal in northern Wisconsin, must decide how to handle a pair of disruptive students. The school is a mix of Ojibwa and white students, but both of the disruptive students are Ojibwa. This case raises issues for new teachers about dealing with student diversity and behavior.

## Case 27.  Organic Lab Is Hell

*Marie C. Milletti and Elva Mae Nicholson, Eastern Michigan University*

A dedicated chemistry professor devotes a great deal of time to a disabled student, only to have the student grieve his grade. At issue are the student's abilities, the professor's investment of time, energy, and emotion, and the institution's experimentation with disability accommodations. How are accommodation and disability related?

## Case 28.  Who's Learning?

*Beverly J. Stratton, Augsburg College*

Well-crafted assignments with worthy goals can sometimes evoke surprising reactions from students. In this case, an assignment that connects the Bible's influence on American culture upsets a Native American student and leaves the professor questioning her motives.

## Case 29.  Dissin' the Prof

*Susan J. Huber, University of St. Thomas*

Diversity as a value in higher education brings with it some tricky problems. In this case, a model professor is confronted by a powerful, ambitious African-American woman who expects university standards to accommodate her life circumstances. Communication is complicated by the student's open disrespect for the professor and the professor's alleged racist attitude.

# Foreword

When I first picked up the manuscript for this volume, I immediately jumped into the cases. The first one I happened to read—Bruce Smith's tale of the "Unpopular Senior Professor"—hit me between the eyes: I'd *seen* the very situation, and watched a department chair botch it...let me tell you what *not* to do!, I said out loud. The second—Richard Jewell's "Too Much Thinking"—stumped me, at first...soon I found myself down the hall showing it to a more experienced colleague...our spirited conversation drew a third, long-time teacher into the office...quickly all three of us were at it.

Which, I take it, is the point of this collection. Cases like these open the door to conversations we need to have about the classroom situations that keep us awake at night, about the endless variety of student situations, about ourselves as teachers. These are typically difficult conversations to have. We cite the press of time, our different schedules, the uniqueness of our classes, but often the real reason we don't talk about our teaching is that, well, it's just not done...there's not permission to talk about it. Stories we do tell, of course, but they're mostly about students (or administrators) and are told to point up life's absurdities. Seldom are they about a real dilemma before us at the moment.

Over the years I've participated in case discussions, written cases myself, and led case discussions with colleagues and students. Their value to me has been twofold. For one, they create concrete contexts within which to test and apply the book knowledge I have about teaching. We all have some knowledge of the research literature on teaching and of statements like the Wingspread "Seven Principles for Good Practice in Undergraduate Education," for example; but only when I confront a "real," case-based situation and have to apply these abstractions do I really know what I think about them.

A second benefit is that case discussions help me uncover the tacit understandings I carry around in my head about what constitutes good teaching, about my proper role and that of students, of what adequate performance means, and so on. It surprises me to learn, sometimes, what my mental model of "good teaching" really turns out to be...and that not everybody else works from that same set of ideas...and that other people's ideas often make more sense than mine. Cases aim to trigger important personal learning of just this type.

The importance of such learning cannot be overemphasized. Stories and narrative are fine in and of themselves: they help us make meaning of experience and they convey community memory. For professionals, however, they are never enough. The art, craft, and science of teaching requires reasoning with causal models, that as professionals we have a theory of our work. Case discussion, stimulating as it can be on its own terms, serves higher callings when it helps us uncover, test, and refashion the theories that guide our work, and when it thereby helps us develop the *everyday* habits of feedback and reflection that mark the work of a professional.

To that end I enter a caution, based on experience. That is, all of us as academics are well trained in the arts of analysis: we can slice and dice a situation till the cows come home. I've been in more than a few case discussions where we filled up the time with brilliant dissections and second-guesses. The missing ingredient was that nobody ever had to say what they themselves would do in the situation...that is, to come to grips with it personally, in the presence of others. This tendency, I believe, short-changes everyone's learning and makes habits of personal reflectiveness less likely as an outcome. A good practice, two-thirds of the way through a discussion, is for everybody to ask themselves, Where do *I* want this situation to end up? How would I get there?

When I've been in groups that put the "I" in the discussion, I'm always amazed at the range of answers that come forth. What then happens is that the group sifts and sorts the various responses; strategies converge as a "wisdom of the group" takes hold. I've never seen it fail that the group's response becomes stronger and wiser than the response thought up by any one of its members.

Which raises a question: if good conversation routinely produces the better response, why doesn't it happen routinely? In the case mentioned above, "Too Much Thinking," it struck me that "Dr. Terrence" initially seemed clueless; what he did to get help wasn't right; but what were his alternatives, actual or perceived? Was there a conversation to be found that would have helped him reach the wiser response? Who, indeed, would you or I have gone to for that help? What, on our campus, stands in the way? Is there an arrangement we could make—it needn't be complicated—that would bring us the conversational or consultative help we'd need when the next "Janice" walked in the door? These questions illustrate how case discussion takes on power: when it leads to practical understandings connected to my (and our) actual work.

Finally, let me pass along another idea: consider using a case or two in this collection with your class. They weren't written with that in mind, of course. But I can vouch that students leap to the bait when they confront a case that means something to them. Several cases in the "about classrooms" section of this book might serve the purpose...that is, they raise questions of faculty and student role, of classroom power and responsibility, of pedagogy, communication, and dealing with difference. Lots of the problems these cases raise, when you think about it, really have to do with different assumptions about role and responsibility; they arise because student and faculty ideas about what should happen in a class aren't the same. The right discussion at the front end of a course, prompted by a case, might be just the ticket for uncovering those assumptions and getting everyone launched on the right foot.

TED MARCHESE
*American Association*
*for Higher Education*

# Acknowledgements

Many people from many diverse institutions helped to make this book a reality. I am most grateful to the authors of the cases in this publication, as well as to the many others who responded to our "Call for Cases," for sharing their professional experiences, insights, and humor. The Case Editorial Board, a volunteer group chaired by Chris M. Anson (University of Minnesota-Twin Cities), began its work four years ago, reviewing each case submission and providing thoughtful and extensive feedback to authors. Other members of this board included Virginia Arthur (College of Saint Benedict), Joel Peterson (Minnesota State Colleges and Universities), Bruce L. Smith (University of South Dakota), and Kathryn Swanson (Augsburg College). Mary Maus Kosir and Michelle Weis, former staff of The Collaboration, managed the Case Project at various times, and Michelle helped compile the final volume. Carol Rutz, a doctoral student at the University of Minnesota-Twin Cities, provided valuable editorial assistance on the final collection, including the short introductions to each section of the book.

Others involved in the Case Project—members of the project planning committee, including Michael Hemesath (Carleton College), Marie McNeff (Augsburg College), David Schodt (St. Olaf College), Steve Simmons (University of Minnesota-Twin Cities), and other case workshop presenters, including Wendy Klepetar (College of St. Benedict), Marion Larson (Bethel College), Cheryl Medearis (Sinte Gleska University), and Jerry Pitzl (Macalester College)—provided additional stimulus for case authors. Pat Hutchings of AAHE and Rita Silverman and Bill Welty of Pace University provided their experience and inspiration. The Collaboration's Board of Directors, including faculty and administrators from at least 30 institutions, rallied around our goal of making teaching more public and using cases to do so.

For funding and organizational support, we thank The Bush Foundation of St. Paul, Minnesota, and above all Humphrey Doermann, its past president, for his deep commitment to faculty development and his faith in The Collaboration. The Minnesota Private College Research Foundation, led by president David B. Laird, Jr., provided space, equipment, and administrative support for this project, as well as a nurturing environment for The Collaboration's evolution as an organization.

Finally, my deepest thanks to Chris, without whose professionalism, dedication, and thoughtful leadership this volume would not have been possible; to my husband Nicholas, whose patience and good humor offer sanctuary from the steady work of change; and to my parents, Gladys and Jacob Kisner of New York City, who instilled in me the love of learning and the appreciation of a good story.

LESLEY K. CAFARELLI

# Introduction

The book you are now holding—*Dilemmas in Teaching: Cases for Collaborative Faculty Reflection*—is the capstone publication of a six-year project to promote more open dialogue about college teaching.

In 1991, The Collaboration for the Advancement of College Teaching & Learning, a regional alliance of colleges and universities that supports and promotes outstanding college teaching, began an intensive effort to raise the frequency and level of campus conversations about teaching.[1] This effort, funded by The Bush Foundation, was a response to our observation that the culture of privacy around higher education's most public activity—teaching—serves to obstruct both individual and collective efforts to strengthen student learning. How can faculty strive to improve their teaching, for example, if there are few opportunities to observe and learn from other professionals or to wrestle intellectually with colleagues about ways to cope with both common and surprising difficulties in teaching? How can colleges and universities fulfill their public responsibility if there is little or no collective knowledge of how teaching is practiced, sharing of expertise, or joint exploration of teachers' impact on student learning? An academic culture that preserves the privacy—even secrecy—of the classroom fosters professional isolation and stifles improvement.

As a consortium of colleges and universities, The Collaboration provides a unique venue in which faculty and administrators can grapple productively with issues that are difficult and even controversial. By framing important issues in the context of current theory and practice, providing a "level playing field" across disciplinary and positional differences, and exploring affective as well as intellectual dimensions of tough issues, The Collaboration seeks to broaden participants' perspectives beyond their particular campus or departmental horizons. By involving participants from very diverse institutions, The Collaboration also aims to stimulate reflection and lasting improvements across the higher education system. Our view is that the most difficult and serious barriers to student learning are systemic, not specific to individual campuses, and have deep cultural and political dimensions.

The Collaboration's effort to increase the frequency and depth of conversations about teaching has involved several different strategies. First among these were a series of

---

[1]Formerly the Bush Regional Collaboration in Faculty Development.

conferences, summer institutes, workshops, and publications focused on two related, controversial issues: the evaluation of teaching (both formative and summative) and the assessment of student learning. These programs served to explore the cultural, political, human, and structural aspects of these issues, as well as a wide range of approaches to them. Our second, concurrent strategy was The Collaboration's Case Project, an initiative designed to promote the use of cases to stimulate more public campus dialogue about teaching.

As Chris Anson's introductory essay explains, cases provide a flexible form of problem-based learning focused on complex, realistic situations. For faculty and administrators, discussing a case about a real or realistic teaching dilemma can stimulate critical thinking, encourage collaborative reflection on individual experiences, and help faculty rehearse responses to potential teaching dilemmas. Writing cases also encourages reflection, creativity, and humor, in addition to documenting genuine stories and experiences. Publications such as this serve as a public repository of work by reflective practitioners, as Donald Schön describes them. In these cases, the authors frame common assumptions about teaching, test those assumptions, and pose a dilemma that requires new assumptions or solutions. Reflective practice is the cornerstone of professional development, as well as the scholarship of teaching.

Beginning in 1991, The Collaboration's Case Project provided an integrated strategy to promote the use of cases. First, we modelled case discussion, beginning with semi-annual preconference workshops using available faculty development cases by Rita Silverman, Bill Welty, and others. The first workshop, led by AAHE's Pat Hutchings, generated over 80 registrations. We also pursued opportunities to use cases, shorter written or videotaped scenarios such as those in the Bok Center's tape *Race in the Classroom,* and even theatre in conference plenary sessions. We produced A. R. Gurney's *Another Antigone* as a deeply affective opening for a conference on power in the classroom, following the play with structured small group discussions. Later, we commissioned an original play exploring the human aspects of evaluating teaching for another conference opening and subsequently produced it as a videotape, *Opening Doors.* Original cases became a regular component of our weeklong summer institutes, crafted to include issues faced by participating campus teams, to provoke a critical assessment of participants' assumptions, and to promote understandings of issues affecting organizational development and institutional change. We taught cases using the "case method" of the Harvard Business School, collaborative and cooperative learning groups, even a jigsaw approach and role-playing.

Second, with the help of Rita Silverman and Bill Welty, we offered two longer workshops on leading case discussions. Workshop participants engaged in tightly orchestrated demonstrations of case-method teaching and worked in teams to prepare and practice case teaching. From the participants at these workshops, we invited individuals to develop and present workshops using cases, including preconference workshops on writing cases and using cases in the classroom. Some presenters went on the road with Traveling Case Workshops on topics like active learning and diversity hosted by member institutions around our region.

Finally, beginning in November 1993, we launched a "Call for Cases," inviting faculty, faculty developers, and administrators from Collaboration campuses to submit original cases for possible publication. Each case was reviewed as a blind submission by an editorial board of faculty peers, and all case authors received substantive feedback on their drafts. Some cases were accepted as is; others were revised, resubmitted, and subsequently accepted. In total, we received and reviewed close to 70 individual cases; this book contains the 29 best.

So, what are the outcomes of The Collaboration's Case Project? First and foremost, I believe that the project achieved our goal of promoting more open dialogue about teaching. Workshops, conference openings, and summer institutes featuring cases have stimulated lively, critically reflective dialogue on subjects as complex and difficult as the politics around the evaluation of teaching. Faculty have responded to the realistic dilemmas posed by cases and have become more public about their personal struggles, more aware of the organizational context for their teaching, and more confident in their ability to respond to critical dilemmas. With the help of cases, faculty and administrators are working together, collaboratively, as reflective practitioners to explore their assumptions about teaching and refine their practice.

Second, "case" has become a household word and common tool for faculty development on Collaboration campuses. I recall vividly the point at which I realized, overhearing a hallway conversation at one of our conferences, that participants were talking about cases as ordinary, familiar tools of professional development; for a majority of those present (including roughly 50% first-time conference participants from our campuses), we no longer had to define what they were. A few months later, case discussions were popping up regularly in proposals for conference sessions.

Third, some of The Collaboration's family of campuses are now launching local initiatives to use cases regularly in faculty development and to integrate case-based teaching in courses ranging from the social sciences to humanities and engineering. As I write, I am aware of at least four college and university grant requests in the works that involve the development of case-based curricula.

Finally, there continues to be a regular demand for Traveling Workshops using cases, a Collaboration program now supported entirely by participant fees, and for cases to use in campus faculty development workshops, brown bag discussions, and department seminars. We hope that this casebook, then, one tangible product of our six-year project, will provide a useful resource for these discussions, as well as encouragement to other reflective practitioners.

LESLEY K. CAFARELLI
*Director, The Collaboration*
*for the Advancement of*
*College Teaching & Learning*

# Part I:
# Resource Materials

# Stories for Reflective Teaching: Using Cases in Faculty Development

*by Chris M. Anson*
University of Minnesota-Twin Cities

## Storytelling and the Improvement of Teaching

Think back to the last time you had a sustained conversation about teaching. Did it begin because you were discussing some new educational research findings with a colleague? Was it fueled by the newest piece of educational theory from a published book?

Or did it start like this?

"I've got a problem, and I wondered if you could give me some advice."

Or this?

"You won't believe what happened to me last semester!"

Or this?

"Oh, that reminds me of something that happened to me a few years ago when I was teaching a new course for the first time."

Although we are trained to believe that expertise in teaching comes from listening to experts, most faculty find that substantive discussions about teaching are much more likely to be rooted in their own experience, and thus take the form of a story or anecdote. As Witherell and Noddings (1991) put it:

> Adults, like children, are natural storytellers, though they have often
> learned to suppress their urge to tell stories as a way of knowing because
> of the theory of knowledge based on "objectivity and generalizability"
> that is so dominant within the Western world.... We take classroom

discourse to be at the very heart of the teaching-learning process, as it
represents the meaning systems mutually constructed by teachers and
their students.... These meaning systems do not occur in social or his-
torical vacuums, but are rendered meaningful to participants according
to both personal and cultural histories and contexts. (3, 8)

Witherell and Noddings' observation reflects a growing interest in using narratives
and realistic accounts of teaching to promote the kind of thoughtfulness that character-
izes the "reflective practitioner" in education (Brookfield, 1995). It also bears witness to
the experience of many faculty developers, who find that groups of teachers they hope
will reflect on and improve their instruction seem far livelier when engaged in activities
that tap into their own experiences and memories of events than when they are "told"
about the latest educational research or teaching methodologies.

On most college campuses, the social life of teachers often revolves around stories
about their classes, students, and programs. While sometimes told for their humor or
shock value, such stories usually come from the need for teachers to talk through specific problems they may be confronting in their teaching: what to do about a hostile student; how to handle a case of collaborative plagiarism; how to act on a perceived issue
of racism in the classroom. When working through such problems, teachers often find
themselves considering broader educational and institutional implications, thus moving
back and forth between concrete experience and abstract concepts and principles.

Not long ago, for example, a teacher relatively new to the profession consulted me
for advice about a problem in his classroom. Early in his linguistics course, he had asked
the students to tell the class about any non-English languages spoken in their recent family histories, to show how even in the upper Midwest, there is considerable language
variety. As he called on the students and listed the languages on the board, his eyes fell
briefly on a young woman obviously of Asian descent. "Spanish," she said, looking
embarrassed. The teacher said "interesting," wrote "Spanish" on the board, and moved
on. Weeks later, at the end of his course, the teacher found a note from the Asian student in his mailbox; the note was a diatribe against his teaching, bitterly criticizing what
the student claimed was his racist attitude toward Asians. She had made up Spanish as
her "familial language," she explained, to drive home the point that she was adopted by
American parents and raised as a monolingual speaker of standard American English—
and that the teacher had falsely assumed she was Asian by looking at her in anticipa-
tion of a response. The teacher was angry and frustrated to think that any of his
students would find him racist, especially when the activity was designed to reflect and
celebrate diversity, and when he hadn't even called on the student and couldn't remember looking at her during the activity.

This teacher's story raises fascinating teaching issues involving diversity in the classroom, the difference between teachers' goals and students' experiences, and strategies
for including students without embarrassing them. In addition, it raises important concerns about how minority students want to be perceived in our classrooms. What
responsibility did the student have to say something right away, instead of waiting until
the end of the course? What might have encouraged her to express her feelings in the
classroom, at the moment when she felt them, so that other students might have benefited and so that the teacher's intentions would not have been misinterpreted? What
issues of power and authority does the case raise—the teacher's power in leading the discussion and asking for personal information; the student's perceived lack of voice in the
classroom, and her sudden, rashly written note at the end of the course; the teacher's

loss of faith in himself after reading her caustic letter? It is because of their immediacy and situatedness that such questions, often rendered abstract and theoretical in the professional literature, come alive in the context of this teacher's classroom experience. And it is for this reason that "cases" about teaching, like those gathered together in this collection, represent a fruitful strategy for faculty collaboration and the improvement of instruction.

## The Nature of Cases

Recent discussions of ways faculty can become more "thoughtful" in their teaching supports a case-based approach to teacher development (Boyer, 1990). At their simplest, cases are stories about classrooms and campuses—narratives that are designed to engage teachers in open discussion, problem-solving, and the inductive learning of teaching strategies. Typically, a case describes, as richly as possible, an actual or very realistic situation to which many participants can relate. By considering the issues in the case, as well as practical ways to deal with the problem at hand, teachers delve into their underlying beliefs, bringing various approaches or theories to bear on the situation.

There is, of course, a difference between the anecdote about my colleague's problem with the Asian-American student and cases like the ones printed in this collection. For him, the situation was not just realistic—it was real. Our discussion had to navigate the troubled waters of his emotions, self-image as a professor, and anger about what he perceived to be an unjustified criticism. His "case" was immediate and alive. But because printed cases are imagined experiences (even if most cases are embellished retellings of real experiences), they are risk-free. While discussions can become quite animated as participants examine differences in their assumptions and beliefs, no one who reads a case needs to go back into the office or classroom where the case occurred and put to the test a specific strategy to solve the problem documented in the case.

At the same time, cases encourage teachers to move beyond the "idea" of an issue by considering it in a particular context. Instead of talking about diversity in the abstract, workshop participants can read a case in which a young Asian-American student accused an unsuspecting teacher of racism. The complexity of the relationship between the specific case and the general areas it brings to the surface of discussion allows for a kind of open-endedness that makes discussions of cases so engaging and unpredictable. In addition, while faculty development efforts often struggle with the variety of experience that teachers in a department or on a campus bring to a meeting or workshop, cases are equally meaningful to all readers. Long-time teachers can draw from years of their own experiences, while newer teachers can relate the case situations to their own ongoing lives in the classroom, building strategic knowledge for how to handle issues that may not yet have confronted them.

Cases and case studies are not, of course, a new invention; they have been used for many years for educational purposes, perhaps best illustrated over the past few decades in the Harvard Business School. Over the last decade, however, cases have become much more popular as a means for faculty development, well illustrated in the development of the Pace University Center for Case Studies in Education, the appearance of various electronic listserves and books of cases (see Anson, et al., 1993), and The Collaboration's own five-year case project, which has culminated in the publication of this volume. Pat Hutchings, director of the American Association of Higher Education's

"Teaching Initiative," identified the case method as a major component of AAHE's project aimed at improving college teaching and learning:

> Serious attention to the improvement of teaching is on the rise on campuses. But what's the best route to improvement? How can faculty be most helpful to one another? What's the most productive way to talk about important pedagogical issues? One answer that looks increasingly promising is *cases*—narrative, story-like accounts of teaching and learning incidents that raise pedagogical issues in faculty discussion. (Hutchings 6)

Cases can take many different forms and be used for a variety of purposes. "Case studies," which are often used in medicine, the law, and business, present actual or highly realistic (and detailed) situations; participants in the case discussions often assess a set of decisions, diagnosis and treatment, or other "outcome" for its validity and wisdom. The case study may even include sometimes conflicting commentary by experts in the field. The object of the case is not so much to "solve" the problem as to see what reasoning led to a particular course of action. "Decision cases" may be more open-ended, but are also usually long and detailed, with multiple sources of information, appended documents, and other materials. Because of their length, such cases may be read and discussed in stages or parts, conclusions about each section paving the way for new material and fresh puzzles.

Cases for faculty development can be relatively short and undetailed, or they may be several pages long and include information about the context that helps to make the case complicated and more interesting. The former type of case is sometimes called a "vignette." Because it includes little detail, it is designed to help participants connect the brief narrative to their own experiences, encouraging the sharing of stories and events. An example of such a vignette is one I wrote titled "Technology Blows a Fuse," which has been used at several of The Collaboration's Traveling Case Workshops.

### Technology Blows a Fuse

For six months, Angela D'Arinzo had been exploring the marvels of electronic mail after her university had become fully networked. From her home computer, she could carry on faculty committee work, get information from the library, send materials to her department office, read the university bulletin, and talk and consult with colleagues all over the country.

Angela soon discovered that many of her students also had e-mail accounts and could use computers to send and receive messages. Excited by the possibility of further reducing her time on campus (which always seemed to slow down her work on important projects), she gave her music history class her e-mail address and urged them to write to her. They soon did, and before long Angela was carrying on many productive "conferences" with students using this medium. As her time on the computer increased, she cut back on her office hours—in part because so few students were coming in for face-to-face meetings, using their computers instead. By staying at home two days a week, she could save almost four hours of commuting time and devote it instead to her work and her increased electronic contact with students.

One day, Duke Cosin, a student in Angela's class, showed up during her office hours. Angela remembered that Duke had complained on the first day of classes about the high cost of the textbooks. Glancing up from her computer screen, she noticed that he seemed concerned. After some cursory greetings, he said, "Let me get to the point, Professor D'Arinzo. I know you like all this computer stuff, but you gotta realize that some of us don't have computers. I know for a fact that the people who are writing back and forth with you are doing a lot better than the rest of us in this class. But I'm poor; I got a wife and kids to feed. Us working people, we can't get any extra help. I just don't think that's fair. I think you should stop all the computer stuff so that these other students don't ruin the curve. Besides, I work all day when I'm not in your class. I can't even make the couple of hours when you're here. I had to take unpaid time off just to come in today!"

In her highly logical way, Angela instantly considered Duke's objection. Were the students who communicated a lot with her really performing better? Come to think of it, the four who she wrote back and forth with the most were the best students in the class...but was that the cause or the effect of their e-mailing her so often?

One hand still on her keyboard, Angela sat, frozen by Duke's words.

## Issues for Discussion

- How should Angela respond to Duke? How do you respond to his claim that he is disadvantaged relative to Angela's use of e-mail?

- Do faculty have a right to decide how (and through what media) to allocate their time for students? In allocating their time, through various media, should they consider issues of economic privilege and access to technology?

- As a faculty member, what experiences have you had about the use of technology as this concerns student use and access? Did any problems arise?

Despite its brevity, "Technology Blows a Fuse" often sparks lively discussions about such issues as the use of technology in instruction, the problem of fairness and equal access to technology, and the appropriate media for contact between teachers and students. But in addition to these general concerns about teaching, vignettes such as this one can also raise important issues of policy and administrative procedure on particular campuses. Discussions can turn to the presence or absence of policies that impinge on the actions already described in the case and those that the discussants are proposing. A policy that requires teachers to hold at least five office hours per week on campus might yield one conclusion about "Technology Blows a Fuse" (that Angela is not fulfilling her obligations as a faculty member); it might just as easily call that policy into question because of the impact of technology on the campus or in education more generally (would the policy act as a disincentive for faculty to use e-mail because it simply *adds* to their existing workload?). When such policy-based issues are discussed openly in the presence of administrators, new ideas can emerge for campus-wide reforms. Because the discussions grow out of an imaginary context, they often lack the sorts of tensions or divisiveness that can cloud faculty meetings about actual bureaucratic and administrative concerns.

Typically, cases for faculty development represent something between the short, generalized "vignette" and the full-fledged case study. Most, like the ones included in this volume, are between one and four pages long, and can be read and discussed in a single sitting, which makes them adaptable to a variety of contexts for faculty development, such as half-day workshops, brown-bag lunch meetings, or retreats. Usually the case will remain unresolved, deliberately ending in a moment of dramatic tension. For faculty, the goal is to work through the case, analyzing its usually complicated situation, raising important issues and implications for teaching and learning, and allowing connections to the wealth of experience the group members bring to the discussion. Because there is no risk in proposing certain courses of action, the cases create strategic knowledge—as well as a greater awareness of pedagogical, administrative, and scholarly issues—that teachers can apply to their own contexts if and when the need arises. This theoretical support for cases is especially important for relatively inexperienced teachers, who may not have worked through some important dramatic moments in their instructional work but would rather be prepared for such moments than caught entirely by surprise.

## Using Cases in Faculty Development: Some Strategies

Cases can be used in many ways to promote faculty development and to help teachers to reflect productively on their own instruction. Although it is possible, of course, to read and reflect on cases alone (in the way one might read a short story or newspaper editorial), cases are by their very nature best used in more social and collaborative settings—formal or informal, carefully structured or loose and spontaneous. Each reader interprets a case uniquely, bringing to it his or her own experiences, beliefs, and ways of noticing certain details. Because cases of the kind included in this volume rarely present solutions or recommendations, different readers almost always offer several courses of action for discussion. Cases are not so much designed to promote consensus as to yield critical reflection, a concept often tied to the development of higher-level knowledge and expertise in the teaching profession (see Brookfield, 1995; Schön, 1983; 1991).

Ideally, cases should bring together teachers at different stages in their careers. Because new teachers may bring limited experience to a case discussion, the situation provided in a case begins to enact what would otherwise remain a fairly generalized problem. For example, asking teachers about uses of technology in the classroom can lead to practical information about setting up e-mail chat lines, helping students explore the Internet, or what programs may be available for computer-assisted instruction in teachers' disciplines. But the issues raised in a case such as "Technology Blows a Fuse" can also help teachers to explore the wider and perhaps less immediate problems of access, equity, and the ways we relate to and with our students. The case, in other words, gives us a kind of window into classroom life that can place both practical and theoretical matters into an actual context.

Mentorship programs are also ideal contexts in which to use cases. For example, mentors and the new teachers whom they are advising can meet in a group session. The case discussions in such sessions inevitably activate the experienced teachers' memories of similar situations, which then not only provide models of problem solving for the less experienced teachers, but also show them the process of moving between experience and reflection. Newer teachers can then use this modeling process as they solve problems in their own teaching.

In setting up a venue for faculty development using cases, it's important to keep a few basic strategies in mind. First, consider the types of participants who will attend, as well as the goals and length of the workshop. Then tailor the session to the participants' needs. Consider some of the following questions:

- Why are you selecting one or more particular cases for this occasion? If the participants are very diverse (for example, from different institutions, disciplines, or levels of teaching), it's a good idea to read possible case selections from the participants' multiple perspectives. If a case seems too specific for a diverse audience, choose something that more participants will connect with. You may want to consider the range of disciplines of the participants, the kinds of campuses they come from (if more than one), the kinds of students they serve, the surrounding culture of the institution, or even the institution's mission. If the situation in the case seems extremely remote from the experiences of the participants, it may still be interesting to discuss the case, but keep in mind that it may not connect very strongly to the group's own current situation.

- How much time will you give to participants to read and formulate some responses to the case? In some formats, for example, participants take a case home between sessions (or are sent the case in advance), along with a list of questions for consideration. Participants may even be asked to write out a response, as is typical when cases are used in graduate courses for teachers. More often, participants will read the case at the meeting, and respond to it before engaging in a large-group discussion. The longer and more complex the case, the more time you need to set aside for reading and reflection. Participants will become frustrated if they are given too little time to read a case—or the discussion will get off to a slow start.

- What will participants do after reading and thinking about the case? Some case workshops move directly from reading to large-group discussion, with the workshop leader facilitating the session, calling on participants, and recording responses. Another good strategy is to put participants into small groups of between three and six or seven members to work through the case. At some juncture, the small groups can reconvene to share their discussions in the larger group. Especially when the case is complicated, the small groups might be given the task of "reporting" back to the larger group, through a spokesperson and/or using overhead transparencies as a visual guide to the group's points. Again, it helps to think strategically about the timing of the small-group work. Too little time can make the session feel rushed and cut off the kind of reflection that the case is designed to promote; too much time can result in a poor large-group follow up or listless, bored groups.

- Will you have everyone working on the same case? Standard cases are best used collectively—everyone reads and responds to the same case. If you are using short vignettes, however, separate groups can read and respond to different vignettes, reporting their discussion later to the larger group (who ideally are provided with copies of all the vignettes for their own reference). After a group reports, comments from the larger group can supplement the small group's opinions, analyses, or recommendations.

- How important is it for participants to discuss the details of the case before moving into interpretation and analysis, or presenting a solution or course of action? Generally, the more complicated (and longer) the case, the more important it is to begin with what participants know, in a factual way, about the case. Having reviewed the particulars and established the facts, the group can then move into a deeper analysis of the problem, its causes, and its implications. Case discussions are usually effective when participants do not leap immediately to a proposed solution.

- Will you frame some questions for discussion, or leave the participants free to come up with their own focus? Many cases include discussion questions, but using these is optional. (In this volume, for example, we have included possible discussion questions for each case, but these appear on a separate page. This placement of the questions is deliberate: workshop leaders can choose to omit the questions, modify them, or simply copy them as they stand for the participants.)

It is useful to carefully consider these and other questions before setting up a case workshop. It helps to have a small team or committee design the workshop, considering ways it can be structured and led that are most conducive to a successful and meaningful experience for all the participants. However, little or no planning may be needed for informal discussions such as brown-bag lunches or self-sponsored teaching groups. In such contexts, the cases themselves are usually interesting and realistic enough to lead to lively discussions.

## Cases: Broader Applications

In addition to occasional workshops, cases can be used for more sustained efforts to promote faculty development. In broader efforts to improve instruction, for example, cases can become one part of a series of activities, workshops, meetings, and documents. Teaching portfolios, which are now being used across the country as a way to encourage both the formative and summative evaluation of teaching (see Anson, 1994; Anderson, 1993; Seldin, 1991; 1994) are ideal sites for responses to published cases. Participants can first discuss cases in a faculty-development workshop, and then write up their own analysis of the cases as portfolio entries.

Cases can also be used as a springboard for participants to describe their own teaching "moments" in story-like or narrative form. Unlike the cases in this collection, such narratives might include the teacher's own analysis of the situation and course of action, thus revealing his or her own reflective practice. This creative process of writing cases about one's own instruction can also encourage teachers to move beyond the particulars of their own situations and consider the broader implications of their teaching. On some campuses, teachers are publishing cases about their own teaching in local faculty development newsletters, which encourages continued dialogue about teaching. (For some strategies for writing cases, see Katherine Swanson's chapter in this collection.)

Finally, cases can be used as one activity in longer workshops on particular topics. To punctuate presentations, discussions, and workshop activities typical of faculty development workshops, cases can offer participants the chance to apply new knowledge and strategies to particular situations—or to deliberately "complicate" and extend new knowledge in order to avoid complacency and a sense that improving teaching is simply a matter of collecting more tools (as opposed to putting them to use to solve complicated situations). In these and other ways, we may find that the use of cases provides a vital new method for the improvement of teaching across a range of institutions.

The cases gathered in this collection represent the work and experience of dozens of teachers at Collaboration institutions. Some have been used in The Collaboration's Traveling Case Workshops, Conferences, and Summer Institutes; many have already prompted lively discussions on campuses across the region. It remains the aspiration of all the people involved in The Collaboration's Case Project that we can continue to tell each other stories about our teaching, whether in case form or just in casual conversation, as a fundamental way for us to reflect on our work and share our experiences for the collective benefit of our profession.

## WORKS CITED

Anderson, Erin, ed. *Campus Use of the Teaching Portfolio: Twenty-Five Profiles*. Washington, D.C.: American Association of Higher Education, 1993.

Anson, Chris M. "Portfolios for Teachers: Writing Our Way to Reflective Practice."

Anson, Chris M., Joan Graham, David A. Jolliffe, Carolyn Smith, and Nancy Shapiro. *Scenarios for Teaching Writing: Contexts for Discussion and Reflective Practice*. Urbana, Ill: National Council of Teachers of English/Alliance for Undergraduate Education, 1993.

Black, Laurel, Donald A. Daiker, Jeffrey Sommers, and Gail Stygall. *New Directions in Portfolio Assessment*, ed. Portsmouth, NH: Heinemann-Boynton/Cook, 1994.

Boyer, Ernest. *Scholarship Reconsidered: Priorities of the Professoriate*. Princeton, NJ: Carnegie Foundation for the Advancement of Teaching, 1990.

Brookfield, Stephen D. *Becoming a Critically Reflective Teacher*. San Francisco: Jossey-Bass, 1995.

Edgerton, Russell, Patricia Hutchings, and Kathleen Quinlan. *The Teaching Portfolio: Capturing the Scholarship in Teaching*. Washington, D.C.: American Association for Higher Education, 1991.

Hutchings, Pat. "Using Cases to Talk About Teaching." *AAHE Bulletin,* April 1992.

Schön, Donald A. *The Reflective Practitioner: How Professionals Think in Action*. New York: Basic Books, 1983.

Schön, Donald A., ed. *The Reflective Turn: Case Studies in and on Educational Practice*. New York: Teachers College Press, 1991.

Seldin, Peter. *The Teaching Portfolio*. Boston: Anker, 1991.

Seldin, Peter. *Successful Use of the Teaching Portfolio*. Boston: Anker, 1994.

Witherell, Carol, and Nell Noddings, eds. *Stories Lives Tell: Narrative and Dialogue in Education*. New York: Teachers College Press, 1991.

# In Case You're Writing a Case: Some Suggestions

*by Kathryn Heltne Swanson*
Augsburg College

Do you think Professor English should change Sam Student's grade? Should Chair French discuss Professor Allons' several negative student evaluations with their dean? Was Adjunct Andy treated fairly when new contracts were issued? Professor History worked hard to ensure student involvement in his revised course syllabus, but worries about covering all the departmental objectives for his survey course...and now he's supposed to add a writing component as well. How can he (and his students) survive?

These scenarios could be the backbones of several cases. Although college faculty members may not readily engage in discussion when general topics such as grading, student evaluations, equity issues, adherence (or not) to a canon, and increased demands to expand course content are present, embedding such issues in the context of a case rarely fails to elicit lively and productive discussion.

Writing and presenting cases to elicit discussion of academic issues, then, is a useful means to enable faculty and administrators to consider everyday problems in credible, yet nonthreatening, situations. By examining many aspects of a case, participants must collaboratively solve problems and practice strategies that are applicable to everyday academic life.

For this discussion process to work optimally, careful construction of such cases is essential. After reading and evaluating many cases submitted for inclusion in this Casebook, I have distilled a few suggestions that may help writers who are beginning or revising cases.

First, be sure that the issue embedded in the case is clear, relevant, and complex enough to generate a full discussion. Such issues as course development, student assessment, faculty evaluation, peer collaboration, interdisciplinary teaching—as well as many others—are matters all faculty consider. In constructing a case, choose one such issue and be sure that the problem/question you have in mind as you write is the same one that readers will also see as a focus of the case. The case should present a dilemma, a dramatic issue, which elicits open-ended discussion ultimately leading to consideration of a more generalized academic problem. Often successful cases have several layers, all connected to the focal issue, for readers to consider.

One of the best ways to be sure that your case is engaging and complex is to construct carefully the conflict, the critical incident. Be sure the conflict is believable and generalizable; it must be something readers are sure has happened or could happen to them at their institutions.

Create characters who experience the conflict, and then work to construct believable dialogue among them. It is usually manageable to write conversations for two or three people, but in the short span of a case, creating dialogue for five or six characters is probably not a reasonable task. Read the dialogue aloud to see if it sounds natural and believable.

Construct the exchanges so that you can avoid as much as possible the "stage directions," i.e., "he said"/"she said." Merely set the scene, alternate paragraphs between two speakers, and let the conversation flow. The key here, as in any effective writing, is to let the speakers *show* the conflict, and thus the larger issue of the case.

Just as cases are successful because they are specific and show rather than tell academic issues and problems, your case will show real faculty members, students, and administrators wrestling with believable academic problems and conflicts.

As you write the end of your case, be sure that you come to some sort of conclusion—perhaps a general open-ended question or several somewhat more specific questions. These concluding questions may be directly stated or left implicit; the key is that they exist. Be sure the questions that emerge are, in fact, embedded organically in the case itself.

Finally, as you finish and revise the case, be sure that you think about principles of effective writing.

Read the entire case aloud and ask yourself these basic questions:

- Is the focus of the case clear?
- Are the paragraphs and incidents presented in a unified way; i.e., free from digression?
- Does the case provide an adequate context, enough detail, for discussion of the larger issue?
- Is the issue sufficiently complex to engage readers in sustained discussion and problem solving?
- Are the critical incident and conflicting characters believable?
- Is the case readable and well-organized; i.e., do transitions move the reader clearly through time changes and scene shifts?
- Is there a logical and consistent point of view?

- Are the verb tenses used consistent?

- Has careful proofreading eliminated any errors of grammar and mechanics?

- Are the case and the issue/dilemma it presents interesting and worthy of discussion?

# Part II:
# Cases About Classrooms

# Introduction

*by Carol Rutz*
University of Minnesota-Twin Cities

Let's daydream for a moment. Let's imagine the classroom as the teacher's theatre: the teacher produces, directs, and stars in a well-crafted production designed to instruct, persuade, and delight. Students, as the audience for this production, eagerly take their seats to drink in truth, beauty, and elegance, whether the subject is Shakespeare or calculus.

After the performance, all rejoice in their new knowledge tempered with nuanced insight. Best of all, disagreements or critical interpretations are based on respectful intellectual positions untainted by envy, jealousy, suspicion, or disappointment. As debate proceeds, even the dissonant chords resolve and echo serenely throughout the ivory tower.

Does this daydream match your classroom experience? Chances are, it doesn't match at all. Nevertheless, as we teachers carefully set our goals and plan our courses, we may delude ourselves with such a vision. No wonder we feel disappointed, or even betrayed, when the real people in our classrooms—including ourselves—intrude into our daydream with problems and distractions we neither anticipate nor welcome.

The cases in this section show several teachers facing situations that cause disruption, confusion, irritation, anger, conflict, and disappointment. In "Critical Thinking or Thinking Critically," Professor Collins' inspiration about using real-life examples of critical thinking backfires. This case shows how classroom roles and other roles professors and students play in the larger community provide a wider stage for testing boundaries and relationships.

Because cases are used in many classroom situations, the methodology promoted in this casebook is also worthy of examination. Note how Dr. Jim Higgins, in "Group Cases: One Professor's Dilemma," finds that his carefully-prepared course design breaks down when his students' personal circumstances affect their availability for and investment in group projects.

In an attempt to use a required course-evaluation procedure as a basis for developing classroom rapport, Sam Trugood and his adult students develop criteria for evaluating his performance as their professor in a Weekend College course. But "Judgment Day" arrives, and the criteria don't seem to hold.

Another case on peer groups, "The Loafing Letdown," reveals a management professor baffled by students' unwillingness to confront one another on poor or indifferent performance. Does this experience doom his course design?

One of the assumptions teachers bring with them to the classroom deals with establishing and promoting respectful treatment for all within that classroom. Sometimes that assumption is challenged in surprising ways. "The Case of the Harassed Teacher" shows Professor Kimako Ashanti's dismay at discovering obscene graffiti labeled with her name and that of a male co-teacher. Is this a teaching issue to be confronted or just an adolescent prank to be ignored?

Teaching occurs in a complex life context for all concerned. In "Yes, Virginia, You're in a Pickle," a junior faculty member attempts to maintain her strong teaching while juggling department political issues that may be complicated by student complaints.

Access to higher education means better employment prospects for students—or does it? In "Too Much Thinking," Dr. Terrence has to decide whether Janice, a single mother, can compete successfully in his course. What does a diploma imply about a graduate's knowledge, skills, and abilities?

The issue of standards comes through in another dimension as Professor Kate Klemmetz tries to maintain rigorous "Grade Expectations" in the face of student dissatisfaction and lack of support from her department chair.

Teaching and learning are almost never politically and ideologically "objective." As teachers, we are often caught between wanting students to see the world the way we do and respecting them for their own beliefs and values. In "The Jonas Incident," a teacher comes face-to-face with a conflict of ideology as she tries to grade a paper she finds to be racist. Her familiar struggle reminds us that classrooms are, to use Mary Louise Pratt's term, "contact zones" where ideologies meet and sometimes clash.

As the curtain rises on this suite of cases, think about how your classroom preparations accommodate the real people who will animate that classroom. Are you ready for surprises?

# Critical Thinking or Thinking Critically

*by James H. Smith*
Northern State University

## ABSTRACT

A political science professor tries to demonstrate his views on critical thinking by writing to the student newspaper and through specific requirements on writing assignments. Students resist his approach, both in and out of the classroom.

## POSSIBLE DISCUSSION QUESTIONS

1. What role does the faculty play in student government elections? Did Professor Collins choose an appropriate role? Why or why not?

2. Look carefully at Professor Collins' critical writing assignment. What are its strengths and weaknesses?

3. Professor Collins lectured to his students about critical thinking. Was this the best way to present the material? Why or why not?

4. What connections, if any, does Professor Collins' piece in the student newspaper have with his political science students' attitude and performance?

5. What suggestions do you have for Professor Collins as he tries to rescue his class and himself from a miserable semester?

# Critical Thinking or Thinking Critically

As students returned to campus for fall semester, campaigns kicked off for student senate and other offices. One candidate, a young woman named Leona, ran a campaign long on hackneyed mottoes and short on substance. Listening to her speak one afternoon in the memorial union, Professor John Collins hit upon what he thought would be a brilliant idea. He took careful notes of her speech and transcribed them. That evening he carefully noted every logical or analytical error in her presentation and wrote an editorial for the campus newspaper exposing the absence of clear thinking in her address. Professor Collins had hoped to breathe new life into his classes this fall with the addition of special assignments dealing with critical thinking, and he planned to use her comments and his analysis, as printed in the paper, to illustrate proper and improper use of critical thinking for his courses that fall.

Soon, practically every student on campus had read his editorial, as it became a *cause célèbre* to those running for office. Whereas Collins had hoped to educate the campus on the importance of critical thinking, most students responded with disgust to what they perceived as yet another example of the faculty acting *in loco parentis*.

"Why can't we run our campaigns without faculty interference?" demanded a letter to the editor.

Leona herself rebutted Collins' challenges by stating, "How dare a faculty dude criticize a student's thinking! If we couldn't think, we wouldn't be here. We are outraged by the faculty's lack of sensitivity to students, and Dr. Collins is especially insensitive!"

Although Professor Collins had high hopes for his ideas on teaching critical thinking, his efforts appeared to have taken an ugly turn. What had started as an initiative to inculcate logical analysis and critical thinking into his political science students seemed to have broken down even before classes had begun.

---

Professor Collins had wanted to find a way to help his students learn how to write and speak logically and to think critically. He chose as the vehicle for this effort the writing and presenting of short summaries of articles found in professional journals of political science and public administration. He required the students to find recent writings on subjects covered in his Constitutional Law, State Politics, and Public Budgeting courses.

On the first day of classes, Professor Collins formally introduced his classes to his concept and explained that the critical analysis component would make up twenty-five percent of their grade. He gave them a detailed format to follow:

Format for the article analyses:

POLS 360 Sect. #
Your name
Date due

**Bibliographic citation of the article.** For example: Lavelle, Marianne. "A System of Failure," *National Law Journal*, April 24, 1989, 1, 33–36.

**Abstract.** Write an abstract of the article in two to three sentences. Use this section to summarize the contents of the entire article.

**Key point.** Identify and discuss the key point of the study. Explain how and why it is significant or important in a political setting. Summarize your comments in one crisp, concise sentence. This section is vital in showing that you can identify the key concepts and thesis of the article.

**Evaluation of the study.** Evaluate the article: be critical but fair. How well did the author(s) make their points? Could this article or study be improved? How? Did the article omit anything you deem important? If so, what? This section should be three to five sentences—make them count!

**Lessons learned.** Summarize what you learned as a result of reading the article. How did it change your mind or perspective about the subject? How can you use this new knowledge at work? Write your comments in one to two sentences, but be careful of just lavishing praise or stating that everyone should read and heed this article.

Since the first assignment was due in a week, he encouraged his students to get started right away. He then launched into what he later realized to be an overly complex discussion of critical thinking, modeling, and hypothesis testing. Several students dropped his course immediately after his lecture ended.

Those who didn't drop came to class the next week, some with papers in hand, others without. While grading the papers that night, it became clear to Collins that his students exhibited confusion over the assignment. For example, instead of a single paragraph abstract, some students continued to summarize the article throughout all four of the required sections. Many others could not identify the *key point* or wrote far more than the single concise sentence that Professor Collins wanted. The *evaluation* paragraphs aggrieved the professor the most. The papers lacked insight, didn't critique the article, or just said something on the order of "I liked it a lot. It was interesting. I'd like to read more about the subject." The *lessons learned* paragraph, the last of the five required parts, contained superficialities or exhibited scant reflection. A wave of nausea wafted over him as he read paper after paper lacking the very characteristics he so desperately longed for his students to acquire.

The next class meeting, Collins returned the papers, many of which contained Collins' stinging remarks, which hurt the feelings of more than a few. He referred a large number of his students to the campus writing center, an act perceived by those so referred as a form of punishment (Dunceville, they called it) and by the writing center staff as an undue inconvenience.

His students, apparently interested and willing to learn at the semester's start, had by now, barely over a week into the semester, become bored, restless, and disinterested in the professor's attempts to teach them something many felt they already knew and many more believed to be some arcane concoction cut whole bolt from Collins' eccentric imagination. Some students got up and left class early that day.

Professor Collins now felt on the verge of panic. He tried to recover by trying to explain in greater detail what he wanted from them on their assignments. He encouraged his students to select articles to analyze that challenged them to reflect deeply; he also suggested they find articles where the students tended to disagree with the author's point of view.

He provided this rationale, "I've a tip for you: your ability to think critically about what you read, analyze what others wrote, and evaluate the articles or studies in terms of your own learning and understanding are imperatives. Until you get the hang of this difficult task, you may want to deliberately select only articles with which you disagree. Writing these papers may be similar to a debate, where the affirmative has a built-in disadvantage. You could benefit by taking the negative regularly, until you are skilled enough to try the affirmative."

"Why would you say that, Professor Collins?" asked one of the students in the back of the room. "Isn't disagreeing all too prevalent, especially on this campus?"

The words clanged as a gong inside his head, and a few students snickered. As he looked at her, he recognized her familiar face: it was Leona, the candidate he had criticized in his now infamous editorial!

Hesitantly, he responded, "Because it's always easier to oppose an idea, especially another writer's; skill in advocating ideas or points of view comes much harder."

To himself, he thought, "What will come much harder for me will be to endure the embarrassment of her presence in my class all semester. Everything I do or say will be filtered through that unfortunate incident."

That evening at home he wondered how to improve the situation. He thought to himself, "Should I continue to bear down on them in these critical thinking assignments, praying that they'll get it? Will professors in general education and in other majors use similar tactics in the classroom to teach thinking skills? Should I throttle back, and make it easier on them (and thereby on myself)?" Collins felt himself in a quandary, compounded by angry and confused students and a concerned administration that noted the sudden decline in enrollment in his classes.

# Group Cases: One Professor's Dilemma

*by Srinivasan Ragothaman*
University of South Dakota

## ABSTRACT

This case features a single mother, a basketball player, and a grading policy adopted by an instructor. This case addresses certain risks associated with using the case method in the classroom. Cooperative learning and grading issues are also highlighted.

## POSSIBLE DISCUSSION QUESTIONS

1.  Professors are understandably frustrated when students fail to read the syllabus and then ask for special favors. Does Jim Higgins' situation seem familiar to you?

2.  Was Jim correct in asking Brian, Bob, and Sarah to work out an arrangement for their group?

3.  What do you think of Jim's handling of the second group's problem? How could he have uncovered and addressed Peter's absences earlier?

4.  Can you propose guidelines for helping professors head off problems like this?

5.  Does collaborative pedagogy invite problems? Why or why not?

# Group Cases: One Professor's Dilemma

A neophyte business instructor, Dr. Jim Higgins, wrote to a dozen colleagues in other universities and obtained their syllabi for a junior-level business course. After examining them, Jim decided to require six cases and administer three examinations for the course. He specifically mentioned this in the course requirements and the grading policy in the syllabus. Major objectives of the course included: cooperative learning, effective oral and written communication, team work, group dynamics, and solving unstructured problems. The cases were worth fifty percent of the course grade and the three exams accounted for the balance. Cases were to be graded on two elements: the written part (eighty percent), and the oral presentation (twenty percent). These cases were to be completed by students working in groups of three. The groups were randomly selected by the instructor. Eighteen students in the class were assigned to six groups of three each. Each of the six groups was chosen to present a case on different days and all three students in a group had to speak ten minutes each. All six groups we required to complete written solutions for all of the cases and hand in a single team-response for each case.

One month into the course, after two cases had been completed, things appeared to be going smoothly—that is, until Jim had a visit from two members of team number 6, Brian and Bob.

Brian said, "Dr. Higgins, I don't know how to say this. I'm going to be frank. The third member of our team, Sarah, is not contributing to the group projects as she should. She has already missed two of the four meetings we've held so far. We can't let Sarah free-ride on our backs."

Jim responded, "Certainly, no one should be rewarded for other people's work. Grades have to be earned—"

Bob interjected, "Dr. Higgins, not only did Sarah miss two meetings, even when she was present at the other two, she was quiet for the most part. There's no way she did any prior thinking before coming to the group meeting."

"Well, let me talk to Sarah and find out her side of the story. Give me a few days and I will get back to you with some answers. Alright?"

Jim set up an appointment with Sarah for the following day. Sarah was twenty minutes late in meeting with Jim, but Jim didn't mention it when she arrived.

He found himself saying to Sarah, "Brian and Bob were telling me that you did not do your share of the group project. Could you explain to me why you missed two of your four scheduled meetings?"

"Well, Dr. Higgins, I'm a single mother who has to take care of two small children. Not only that, I commute nearly one-hundred and twenty miles every day just to attend classes. It is very difficult for me to meet classmates outside of class hours."

"I see. Yet these hardships do not justify missing your share of the group work. On the first day of the course, when I handed out the syllabus, you were notified of the requirement to complete six group cases, weren't you?"

"I know. But given the fact that I'm a commuter and a single mother with major responsibilities, can't you excuse me from the group cases? I am perfectly willing to complete individual case projects in place of group work. Would you please consider that?"

"Let me think about this. Before I make up my mind, I'd like to talk to Bob and Brian. Is that alright?"

"Okay, I'll check with you next week, Dr. Higgins."

Jim summoned Brian and Bob and said, "I talked to Sarah yesterday. You see, she is a commuter and a single mother with major parental responsibilities. She requested to be dropped from the team. Instead of group cases, she would like to do individual projects. What do you think?"

Bob responded, "Dr. Higgins, that would leave our team with only two members. We will be at a great disadvantage compared to the other five groups, who have three members each."

"That's true, Bob. If Sarah were to do individual projects, she would not benefit from group discussions and cooperative learning opportunities. That would defeat my course objectives."

Brian interjected, "Dr. Higgins, you told us on the first day that we have to do six cases for fifty percent of the grade. How can you break your own rules in the middle of the course?"

"What you say makes sense, Brian. If I show special favor to Sarah, I would be opening the door for all kinds of requests from other students. Someone else might have a problem with an exam and want to write a paper instead. We're back to square one. What else can we do to resolve this?"

Brian responded, "You're the professor, Dr. Higgins. Why don't you give us an answer?"

Jim smiled and said, "Well, this problem belongs to your group, folks. You two have to talk to Sarah and come up with an acceptable solution. Good luck!"

Bob, Brian, and Sarah got together and reluctantly decided that Sarah would give her written answers to the other two team members for the remaining four cases, and they could write the group response after seeing her answers and completing their own discussion. Sarah would attend the group's meetings when time and circumstances permitted.

After two months had gone by and all the cases had been completed, Jim received a visit from two members of group number 4, Jane and Julie. They had a complaint about Peter, a basketball player, the third member of their team.

Julie said, "Dr. Higgins, we have a problem with the input provided by Peter. Peter missed almost thirty percent of the team meetings, and even when he was present, his contribution was next to nothing."

"Why did you wait so long to voice your feelings? It's almost the end of the semester."

Julie responded, "Well, since he's a popular basketball player, we kind of felt intimidated."

"Why are you complaining now?"

"Well, now that finals are around the corner, we're concerned about our grades. So we decided to come and talk to you."

"I see."

Jane added, "Dr. Higgins, you assigned a less-than-average student to our team. It's not fair to give the same grade to all three of us for the written part of the cases."

"Groups were chosen randomly, Jane. Sometimes you get bright team members, other times average ones. This is exactly the kind of situation you will have to deal with in the real world!"

"Well, Dr. Higgins, that might be. But the fact remains that we received very little input from Peter. Some of the other teams who had better students got more points than we did."

"I will agree that there are drawbacks inherent in this system. While there may be a few point differences between teams of these group cases, I'm not sure how it will affect anybody's letter grade. You'll each have to take three individual exams. Anyway, let me talk to Peter and hear his side of the story."

Jim summoned Peter and said, "Peter, Jane and Julie were here yesterday to see me. They were telling me that you were absent for thirty percent of the group meetings. Is that true?"

"Dr. Higgins, my absences were unavoidable. I'm on the varsity basketball team and when we play away games, I have to go out of town. I can get a letter from the coach if you want."

"That won't be necessary, Peter. I read the student newspaper and know you had several away games this season. When you went to the team meetings, were you fully prepared and ready to contribute?"

"Of course, Dr. Higgins. I always do the best I can."

Jim heard himself say, "Thank you, Peter."

On his way home that evening, Jim was thinking, "Maybe I should have kept a closer watch on these groups and asked them every now and then if everything was alright. It is much easier to prevent problems before they occur, rather than solve them afterward."

# Judgment Day

*by Marie McNeff*
Augsburg College

## ABSTRACT

This case involves a professor and adult learners in a weekend college introductory philosophy class who jointly decide on criteria by which the professor will be evaluated. The students then judge the professor on what seems to be a different set of criteria. The student evaluations result in reprimands by the department chair and academic dean.

## POSSIBLE DISCUSSION QUESTIONS

1.  Why do you suppose there was a mismatch between Sam's expectations for his students' evaluations of him as a teacher, and the evaluations themselves?

2.  What other means do teachers have at their disposal to encourage students to decide how the teacher is to be evaluated? What are the potential risks and benefits of these methods?

3.  If you were Sam, would you have done anything differently in the meetings with the chair and the dean?

4.  How did trust between students and faculty enter into this case?

5.  What are the risks and benefits to evaluating collaborative learning in a course?

6.  What were the students' criteria for Sam, and how reasonable were they?

# Judgment Day

Saturday morning it was raining. It also was the first day of school at a small liberal arts college located in a rural area of the upper Midwest. Sam Trugood walked from his parked car to his classroom, agenda in hand, to begin the first session of Philosophy 204. Sam had been teaching for six years now but still felt an electric charge the first day of class. He felt it was important to make a good impression on the students.

The course was an offering through the Weekend College, and consequently, the students were mostly adults returning to school. Adults represented an especially challenging group of students for Sam, as their expectations were often different from younger students. Sam knew that many of his students would be older than himself. At first, this fact daunted him, since as a child he was always taught to respect his elders. However, he had come to terms with the situation and had taken classes on how to teach adult learners. Adult learning theory said that it was important to set a tone of collaboration and responsiveness with the students. This tone was his goal for the first day of class.

When he stepped into the room, he saw about twenty-five students awaiting his arrival. The students, all sitting quietly, their eyes fixed on Sam, did not seem to know each other, judging from the lack of conversation among them. The room was a well-lit, spacious area in Old Main, which used to be the student center in years past. True to his belief in active learning, Sam introduced himself and then immediately arranged the students in groups of three and asked them to introduce themselves to each other and talk about what they expected out of the course. Each small group would then report on their list of expectations. The purpose of this activity was to help him get an idea of what students anticipated from the class and to see if he needed to make some adjustments to the course content.

As the groups reported, Sam realized that most of the students were interested in applying information gained from the class to their work situations. This was not a surprise, but it required a definite deviation from the way a typical introductory philosophy course was presented. However, Sam felt he was up to the challenge, and he decided to include more about ethics and about how one metaphysically understands good and evil in the phenomenal world.

Having disposed of the question about class content, Sam turned his attention inward by asking the class, "How are you going to determine if I am a good teacher? On what criteria will you judge me as a teacher in this course?" Sam had learned from previous classes that many adult learners had well-defined criteria about what they expected from a teacher. This was the first time he had taken this approach for those criteria, but it seemed reasonable that he should consider the students' expectations in creating a good learning environment.

One student responded quizzically, "What do you mean, on what criteria will we judge you as a teacher?"

Sam replied, "At the end of this course, you will be asked to evaluate me. What do you expect of me as a teacher? Again, working in small groups, I would like you to identify criteria on which you will judge me as a teacher. This will help me to create a climate that will help you to learn."

Many students seemed enthusiastic about being able to express up front what they liked in a teacher. Some, however, thought it was a trick question. After the initial reactions and discussion, the groups agreed on ten main criteria they thought were important in evaluating a professor:

- respect us and recognize us as individuals, not as a group of adult learners
- help each of us to succeed
- recognize all the knowledge and experience we bring to the class
- give specific feedback to our assignments
- show how abstract ideas relate to what we do in our lives
- explain what is expected for each of the assignments
- give us handouts on things we are supposed to remember
- treat us like adults, not like children
- be on time
- allow us to talk and to discuss in class

Once the class had agreed to these expectations, Sam tried to live up to them in the way he led the course. During the semester, he posted the expectations above his desk as a reference. At the end of each class period he spent a few moments asking the students to write what had gone well for them in the class and what could be improved. He was monitoring the class sessions to avert any major problems from building up without his awareness.

The final day of the course came, and course evaluations were distributed. As was the college policy, Sam left the classroom to ensure students' anonymity. The students' opinions of the course were collected, placed in an envelope, and delivered to the Academic Dean's office by one of the students.

On December 15, two weeks after the course was over and grades were turned in, Sam found a note in his box asking him to meet with the department chair, Dr. Molly Reinhold, at 2:00 on Wednesday to discuss the results of the course evaluation. Sam, knowing the care he had taken at the beginning of the class to assess the students' expectations of him as a professor, looked forward to the meeting.

Wednesday was a cold and rainy day; a cool breeze blew from the north. Dressed casually in a sweater, Sam shielded himself from the elements. He arrived at Molly's office shortly before his 2:00 appointment, and she greeted him with small talk about the onset of cold weather and how it was nice that the quarter was finally over. She then rose from her desk, closed the door, and proceeded to retrieve the overall class rating of Sam's course from a plain brown envelope.

"It appears that students were quite dissatisfied with the course," she said, handing the ratings to Sam. "Three major areas of discontent were evident in the evaluations. Generally, they thought you used assessment techniques that were inappropriate. They were disappointed that you expected preparation outside of the course time period. They also expected you to know everything or almost everything about philosophy, but it was not apparent to them that you did. They said that the class was not very structured—too much free discussion.

"Sam," she continued, "you know the importance of making students happy in this day and age of the competitive student market. It's important that a positive image of course offerings be held throughout the university. We can't allow this to continue. You must be more in tune with your students or you will not make it as a professor here."

Sam was dumfounded by her comments and felt betrayed and angry. Was this judgment day? He started to defend his teaching strategies but found his emotions taking over his rational thought processes. He excused himself and walked out of Molly's office to think. He had so carefully identified with the students the criteria on which he was to be judged. The comments and evaluations hadn't even addressed the criteria they had worked on the first day.

The students' responses made no sense to him whatsoever. In past classes where he hadn't asked the students to make a list of criteria, things had gone very well. What had gone wrong here? Was there a failure of communication? Sam couldn't believe that his students hadn't lived up to their end of the bargain. It was almost as if they had lost respect for him as he had given them more power to control their own destiny in the class. He knew that a teacher was a fine blend of a friend and a leader, and that sometimes a teacher must "sting" students to prod them to do their best.

It was amazing that the students didn't feel he had shown a mastery of the subject. Sam had tried to promote discussions of subjects while shaping their content, instead of being didactic and telling people only what he thought on the subject. The students must have taken that approach to mean that he didn't know his subject.

After reflecting on these matters for awhile and chatting with one of his colleagues, Sam decided that he was not going to take this criticism lying down. He made an appointment with the academic dean of the college to go over the evaluations and the conversation he had had with the department chair. Essentially, however, the dean repeated the reprimand issued by the department chair. Sam walked out of the office, abashed by what he was hearing. Had the student evaluations become so all-powerful in the college that they now governed and controlled his life as a teacher? Didn't he have rights in the classroom? The students had agreed on a set of criteria to make judgments about him, and they had betrayed that trust.

When he set out criteria to make judgments on assignments, he felt an obligation to follow those criteria, unless he informed students well in advance of a change. How was his obligation any different from the students' obligations to follow their criteria to evaluate his teaching?

Three weeks later, the spring semester started. Snow now covered the ground. The roads were slippery and people walked hunched against the wintry season. Sam had had a good Christmas, but thoughts of his previous semester weighed heavily on his mind. During the holiday break, he had revamped his teaching approach and was ready for the first day of class.

Sam parked his car and walked briskly to Old Main, where his class met. The familiar electric charge passed through his system as he entered the classroom. He addressed the class: "Hello, my name is Professor Sam Trugood. This is Philosophy 204, and if you are in the wrong room please leave now. In this first class, I would like to tell you exactly what I expect of you as students and exactly what you can expect of me as your teacher. Please turn to the syllabus...."

# The Loafing Letdown

*by Ronald A. Klocke*
Mankato State University

## ABSTRACT

A new assistant professor of management finds that student teams are plagued by varying levels of participation and commitment. The issue is complicated by surprising ratings on their peer evaluations of group work.

## POSSIBLE DISCUSSION QUESTIONS

1. Discuss alternative ways to deal with disgruntled team members.

2. Discuss alternative techniques of obtaining a more accurate evaluation of individual team members.

3. Discuss suggestions as to how to handle the immediate evaluation dilemma since the students are gone and a fair evaluation must be made immediately.

# The Loafing Letdown

Tim Fox sat in his office at the end of fall term ready to assign student grades. He gazed at the beautiful maple tree outside his window that was now laced with the first snowfall. His thoughts returned to the beginning of fall term when he could remember the bright green leaves on the tree, the warm weather, the challenge of beginning a new job and seeing the enthusiastic faces of students in his very own classes. His thoughts began to deepen as he reflected on the team members' evaluations of the past term and wondered out loud, "What can I do to solve the current problem and how can I avoid this same dilemma next term?"

Tim Fox was a new Ph.D. and Assistant Professor of Management at Midstates University. Since he was fresh out of graduate school, he was looking forward to his first quarter as a full-time professor in junior-senior level classes. He had some limited experience as a teaching assistant in graduate school but was never responsible for setting up an entire class and evaluating students.

Fall term was fast approaching and Tim had been thinking about the outstanding classes he had as a student as well as those instructors he felt were distinguished. Tim wanted to incorporate the best teaching-learning techniques he had experienced as a student in hopes that someday he would be cited as "outstanding" himself. Tim thought of the long tradition of the usage of cases as a learning device in business education and decided that he would definitely incorporate them in his Principles of Management class. He had many fond memories of his previous experience with case analysis and his meetings with his case analysis team to share ideas for solving the assigned case, developing alternative explanations, and applying the text and lecture material. Many lasting friendships had developed from those team meetings along with some good collaborative learning of the materials. Tim finally decided that case analysis would count one-third of the points toward the final course grade.

His syllabus described the case analysis as follows:

> Each team will analyze the four cases listed below. The first case will be due at the end of the third week of the term, the second at the end of the fifth week, the third at the end of the seventh week, and the fourth at the end of the ninth week. Depending on the size of the class, either one or two teams will present their findings to the class in an oral presentation, in a knowledgeable, professional, and enthusiastic manner. The oral presentation will be evaluated according to the above criteria and each member of the team must contribute to the presentation. Transparencies for use with an overhead projector will be highly valued. All work associated with the assigned case is due at the beginning of the class on the date specified.

> Three of the assigned cases will be written up formally according to the rational model of case analysis. These are not to exceed five pages in length. Each team will hand in a total of three cases for formal presentation and evaluation—the case presented orally to the class plus two of the other four listed to be selected by the team members. All members of the team will receive the same grade for the written papers.

> Consequently, at the end of the course, a peer evaluation will be done to help determine the degree of interest, effort, and participation produced

by each individual member of the team. The remaining case must be handed in by the team for check-off purposes. Other cases will be assigned on a weekly basis for individual and class discussion.

The first week of class, Tim indicated that case analysis teams were to be formed by the first class period of the next week. Students could generate their own team or the instructor would randomly assign students to a team until all class members belonged to a five-person team.

The first case was due the end of the third week of the term. All of the teams handed in their cases on time; two teams presented their analysis orally to the class and some moderate discussion followed. After evaluating the written cases, Tim was slightly pleased by the early results even though the team reports suffered from the typical first-time case analysis problems. Two weeks later when the second case was due, similar results occurred with some slight improvement in the written outcomes. Tim was beginning to feel that his students were getting the hang of case analysis and that the shaping process was taking hold. He felt that all that he had experienced of case analysis as a student was also being experienced by his students. He concluded that all of his students were actively participating in this part of the learning process and that team case analysis would be a continuing part of all of his classes.

Beginning five days before the third case was due during the seventh week, individual students from four of the ten teams came to Tim's office to complain that not all of the team members were participating equally in generating the case analysis. Complaints ranged from team members missing the meetings, to persons not being prepared to discuss the case, to some team members saying that only two of the five persons actively participated in the case analysis and final write-up.

One student, Linda, was particularly vocal in her displeasure with her team members when she said, "I'd like to get an A in this class and that can only be done if I get the cooperation of the other members of my team. Professor Fox, I've had to call two members on several occasions when other team members were already meeting to work on the case. I was only able to connect with one person and he gave some excuse about needing to spend some time on a flight simulator for his aviation class. He did not help one bit on case two. On case one he attended one of our meetings and then all he did was sit there because he didn't even read the case. I'm very frustrated and getting angry!"

Christopher, from another team, said, "Two of our five members handed us about one-half page of useless notes they thought could be used in the case analysis and then said they had to go to their part-time jobs off-campus during our meeting times. It just doesn't seem fair that they should get full credit on the cases when the rest of us end up doing all of the work."

Tim found that to be the general complaint—that all team members wanted to get full credit for the report even though they had not participated equally in its generation. After hearing these complaints he thought to himself, "I must have structured this part of my course poorly, or maybe I've done a very poor job of explaining the team-work approach to my students."

Tim was moderately disappointed in himself and his students and pondered over the solution. He suggested that the students who came to his office not include those team members' names on the cases where individuals had not participated actively. Tim sensed some reluctance on the part of the irritated students to follow his suggestion and he sensed that they felt it was the instructor's obligation to lower a nonparticipating student's grade. He also suggested to the complaining students in his office, "Now is an opportune time for you to apply some of the management and motivation theories we have been discussing in class. Before you begin the last two cases, sit down as a group and confront those members who are not contributing and indicate the consequences if their past behavior continues. Also, remember from the syllabus, at the end of the term each team member will be able to evaluate the other members on an objective appraisal instrument that will take into account individual effort in group activities."

At the next class session, Tim shared these comments with the entire class and felt by their reactions that this should take care of the problem. The last two cases were completed with some team members still filing similar complaints, and Tim responded consistently as he had in the past.

After the last case was finished, Tim handed out the "Group Participation Evaluation" form to his class. With all of the complaints that he had received regarding the varying participation rates of persons on several of the teams, Tim expected some very low individual participation scores for some students. After summarizing the scores in his office, Tim was shocked at the results! Not a single student had received a group participation score of less than 85 out of 100 in the "Good Performance" range on his scale. In fact, several of the forms had written comments on them stating, "The entire team worked well together" and "This group was the best I've worked with in a long time." He thought "How could this be, given the number of nonparticipating complaints from several of the teams?"

Tim wondered how he would be able to assign a fair grade to this part of the total evaluation since the information he had obtained on individual participation in team work was not a true evaluation of what actually had happened. These results had shaken his belief in the future value of team case analysis. He sat back in his chair and stared out his window, wondering how he could ever give his students a fair evaluation.

# The Case of the Harassed Teacher

*by Tony Filipovitch and Mary McDearmon*
Mankato State University

## ABSTRACT

A woman teacher finds offensive graffiti in her classroom and tries to enlist her male co-teacher in a confrontation strategy. Issues of gender, power, and responsibility for a safe teaching environment come bubbling up as they consider the options.

## POSSIBLE DISCUSSION QUESTIONS

1. Do you agree with Professor Ashanti's assessment of the desk graffiti? Are the pictures a form of sexual harassment? Why or why not?

2. After a weekend of rumination, Professor Ashanti telephones Professor Phillips, her co-teacher, first thing Monday morning. This is the first he hears of the problem. How do both of them contribute to misunderstanding?

3. Name the levels of power and the gender roles associated with those levels. Who is most and least powerful in the situation? Professor Ashanti? Professor Phillips? The students? The Dean of Students? The Tenure and Promotion Committee? Other institutional authorities? Academic freedom?

4. If you agree with Professor Ashanti that she should find a way to confront sexual harassment, how would you advise her? If you disagree with her, how would you try to persuade her to let the matter drop?

# The Case of the Harassed Teacher

Students in Professor Kimako Ashanti's course on "Human Relations in Management" were presenting their research to the class, so she sat in a chair-desk in the back of the room. As she listened, she glanced down at the table desk surface, which was covered with graffiti. With a start, she realized that a particularly obscene drawing had her name under it. Embarrassed, she looked away, only to find that the unoccupied desk next to her was also illustrated—with references to a male colleague who team-taught an introductory course with her in that room at another hour.

When the presenting students finished with their papers and class was dismissed, Professor Ashanti pushed the two offending desks into a far corner and went home for the weekend.

All weekend she kept coming back to the problem. There was no doubt in her mind that this was sexual harassment. Whoever had done this had created an intimidating classroom environment. Unlike most cases, this time a student had done it to the teacher.

Her first impulse was to clean the desk tops and pretend nothing had happened. She realized, however, that this was a response of silence. As much as she disliked admitting it, hers was a traditional female response that only perpetuated the harassment. What if she confronted the class? Well, she told herself, the perpetrator could hide in anonymity. Others might deny the problem by saying, "Someone in another class did it," or they could label her "an over-reacting bitch."

Ironically, she had just been teaching the students in her human relations class the importance of standing up to harassment—sexual or otherwise. She had listed for them the sanctions an organization could face if its managers failed to respond to harassment. She had to face it: As a teacher, she was the manager of her class. She could not simply hope the problem would go away.

First thing Monday morning, Professor Ashanti picked up her office telephone. With a sigh, she dialed the number of her co-teacher in the intro class, Professor Gyorgi Phillips.

"Hello," yawned Professor Phillips, a man who didn't much care for Monday mornings.

"Gyorgi, it's Kimako. I need your advice."

"Advice? Um, sure. What's up?"

"It's kind of a long story, but the nub of it is that I have discovered some obscene graffiti on two desks in our classroom—"

"Give it a rest," interrupted Gyorgi. "What these adolescents doodle during our lectures is no business of ours. Besides, that room is busy all day. The offending artists are probably someone else's students."

"Gyorgi, please listen."

This time, her tone got Professor Phillips' attention. "Okay," he replied. "You sound pretty upset. What's the deal?"

"The drawings on those two desks have captions: your name and mine." Professor Ashanti paused for effect.

"Hmmmm," mused Professor Phillips.

"You may think that's just adolescent acting out, and on one level, I agree with you. But in the context of our course, it's more than that. That student—or students—it could be a bunch of them, I suppose—what they're doing is sexual harassment and I'm not going to stand for it!"

Professor Phillips considered his words carefully. "I can understand why you're upset. This must have been disturbing for you to find. And I guess I can see how you could construe it as sexual harassment, but—"

This time Professor Ashanti interrupted. "Believe me, I have thought about this all weekend, and I came close to saying nothing—not even to you. But the more I thought about that, the more I realized that I can't be an honorable teacher—much less a role model as a manager—if I don't take action. If I don't confront this behavior in my own class, what kind of credibility do I have?"

"I see what you mean, and I agree that we have to be willing to practice what we preach, even when we hope we won't have to. But what will a confrontation accomplish? Why would the students admit their guilt? And even if they do, what can you do besides publicly shame them? Please don't forget that another one of our responsibilities as role models—or managers, if you prefer—is to work out problems in a constructive way. Where's the gain in this situation?"

Professor Ashanti was angry, but she knew her colleague had a point. "Okay, Gyorgi. Okay. You're right, I don't want to just expose the guilty person—or people—and ridicule them."

"Good, Kimako," purred Professor Phillips. "I'm glad you see it my way. Let's just let these little creeps think they got away with their naughtiness, and we'll just—"

"Wait! Maybe this is a 'teachable moment'—the kind of conflict that's really an opportunity. Maybe we can show how this rather ordinary naughtiness, or bad judgment, or disrespect—whatever we want to call it—how this kind of common behavior counts as sexual harassment, which is a serious matter. This is a perfect example of how 'boys will be boys' can really harm someone."

Professor Ashanti could feel her interior pain melting away. Just the thought of making this experience into a useful classroom example restored her confidence and erased her dread of facing that class in a few hours.

She went on, eagerly, "We could frame the whole thing with another kind of exercise—you know, a hypothetical situation that would be similar, but not identical to this one. Then if the discussion proceeds as we would expect—after all, our students are likely to try to show they have learned what we've taught them about harassment in the workplace—we can reveal the truth. We can see how they respond to the fact that the situation is not just drawn from life, but from our classroom itself. This could be really great!"

"Hang on, Kimako." Professor Phillips adopted his most professorial tone. "I certainly want to support you in this, but I'm not so sure this really is a 'teachable moment.' To set up the hypothetical story and then spring it on them as their story strikes me as manipulative—perhaps dishonest. All it will get you is a batch of surly course evaluations. And to be blunt, I'm not the one who's vulnerable to student ratings. I have tenure. You don't."

"WHAT?!!" Professor Phillips held the receiver away from his ear as Professor Ashanti shrieked. "Just how does my confronting sexual harassment damage my case for tenure? I'm sure the Tenure and Promotions Committee would love to know that you see them as co-conspirators in a network of silence—people who would endorse the abuse of junior faculty. People who don't want women to speak up for themselves. Are you crazy?"

Professor Phillips' head ached. This Monday was starting out very badly indeed. "Kimako," he said quietly, "I knew when you called that you were upset. Somehow, I've made things worse. I'm sorry. Let's teach class today as we planned. Afterward, you can show me the graffiti and we can talk some more about what to do. Maybe we should get the Dean of Students involved. I don't know. But can we work on it after class?"

Professor Ashanti simmered. "I'll see you in class," she said primly and hung up.

Professor Phillips slowly replaced the receiver. "She's a good teacher, but she's really thin-skinned." He shook his head and reached for the *New York Times*.

# Yes, Virginia, You're in a Pickle

*by Mary R. DeMaine*
College of Visual Arts

## ABSTRACT

A junior faculty member re-applying for promotion tries to put student complaints and a colleague's sabotage into perspective. The faculty member's strong teaching and service to the department were misread by a previous review panel. Consequently, she must undo the damage from the unsuccessful review to make a successful case this time.

## POSSIBLE DISCUSSION QUESTIONS

1. Why is Virginia so distracted?

2. What do you think happened to T.J.'s exam? How would you find out the truth of the matter?

3. Virginia is worried about complaints from students she considers goof-offs. She is also worried about a longtime vendetta waged by a senior member of her department. Should she confide in someone? If so, to whom would you direct her?

4. If you were the dean or a member of the Personnel Committee, how would you advise Steve, the department chair, to work with Virginia and Naureen?

# Yes, Virginia, You're in a Pickle

"I couldn't be in class on Friday." T.J.'s voice sounded more apologetic than he'd planned. "I heard you handed back the midterms, and I was wondering if you brought the ones that didn't get picked up to class today."

Virginia shook her head. "Nope. Meet me in my office after class, and I'll get yours for you."

"I was sick on Friday," T.J. lied.

"Be sure you get notes from someone."

"I'd give him mine," offered Jason, "but I was sick too." Carefully avoiding Virginia's eye, Jason exchanged glances with T.J., his roommate. Both had skipped class on Friday specifically to make the point that they thought it was stupid to take attendance in a college course.

Virginia closed her briefcase. "I'll see you in my office in five minutes, T.J."

Virginia headed out the door, immediately forgetting about T.J., Jason, and their buddies. They were brats sometimes, but they really didn't bug Virginia all that much. She sometimes wondered if they belonged in college, but until they flunked out or decided to take their homework seriously, they were in her class, for better or worse.

No, what was really on her mind had little to do with immature students. Next week her promotion appeal would come before the Personnel Committee. She had plenty of reasons to expect a positive result, but, she reminded herself, she thought she was in good shape last year and—

"So where's my exam?" T.J. had somehow beat her to her office door.

Virginia thought to herself, "I must have been daydreaming." Then aloud, she said, "Just a second, T.J. I have them all in one place." As he settled into a chair, she flipped through the folder of unclaimed exams. His wasn't there. She took the pile out and looked again. No exam. She tried not to panic. Sure, she'd had a lot on her mind, but she didn't think she was so out of it that she'd lose a student's exam.

T.J. cleared his throat. "I'm graduating this semester—if I pass your course."

"Good for you," remarked Virginia dryly. "T.J., I don't see your exam here. Let me check the grade book. Oops—I don't see any indication that you turned it in. I checked off every exam I received, and there is no check mark by your name."

"That's impossible!" T.J. stood up and leaned over Virginia. "Not only did I turn in the exam, I think I did extremely well on it. I studied all weekend for that sucker."

Virginia looked him in the eye. "I don't have an exam for you." She had a vague recollection of hearing T.J. talk about going out of town the weekend before the exam. If she could remember that, why couldn't she remember reading his exam—or not reading it?

Sensing that Virginia was becoming defensive, T.J. persisted. "You must have lost it."

"I don't know how I could have lost it, as I have each student put his or her exam in my briefcase, which goes directly from the classroom to my office. Yours isn't here." Although she tried to sound confident, she had to admit she really couldn't remember whether she'd seen T.J. put his exam into her briefcase.

"I can give you the names of at least six students who'll swear I took the exam."

Virginia stifled an impulse to list T.J.'s soul mates for him. They were the kind who would stick together, no matter how ridiculous the story. She tucked the unclaimed exams back into their folder and gestured toward the door. "I'll have to look through my office and my desk at home. Check with me on Wednesday."

"What are you going to do if you don't find it? I'm supposed to graduate next semester."

"Don't worry about that until I look again. If necessary, I suppose I could have you take a different exam."

"That's not fair! I already aced this one and you lost it!"

"You don't know that, T.J. And I have no record that you took the midterm, much less 'aced' it. We'll have to talk about this after I look once more. I'll see you Wednesday." Virginia turned away, hoping T.J. would take the hint and leave. For some reason, he did.

Virginia closed the door after him, kicked off her shoes, and sank into her desk chair. The more she thought about it, the more convinced she was that T.J. was bluffing. The little stinker hadn't taken the midterm at all. Oh, well. She'd look again, as she'd promised, then offer him a chance to take a similar test. If he put up a fight, she'd refer him to her department chair.

But was that such a good idea? Once again, the promotion issue crowded out all other problems. Rather, it magnified even the most trifling conflict, making everything seem significant. T.J.'s beef about the "lost" midterm added to Jason's objection to the failure on that summary assignment—why should she have to defend an F on a ten-sentence summary of material that covered two hundred years? And this from a guy who had failed the course (although taught by someone else) last year? Another ridiculous situation. But would Steve, the department chair, or the Personnel Committee members look at these two weird cases and find a pattern?

So what if they did? Virginia did have a reputation for being a tough grader and a stickler for details like attendance, but her course evaluations were always very high. Students were asked to rate each professor on several criteria every fall semester, using a range from "well above average" to "above average" to "below average" to "well below average." Consistently, for the past three years, she received no more than a handful of ratings in the average category and never more than one or two in the below or well below average categories. Ninety-nine percent of her ratings had been in the top two categories—most in the highest.

Ah, but student evaluations were only part of the picture. Pesky dissatisfied students like T.J. and Jason were another part. More important, though, were the departmental politics. Here Virginia had less success reassuring herself. Most of her colleagues were at least cordial. Some were congenial, and a few had become close friends over the last three years. But one, Naureen, had been suspicious of Virginia from the beginning. Then one misunderstanding after another—well, one conflict after another would be more accurate, thought Virginia.

Virginia pulled out a lower desk drawer and put her feet up. How did that mess with Naureen get started? If she'd had to date it, Virginia would have put the beginning of their mutual problem at a year before Virginia's application for promotion. Naureen was on sabbatical, and while she was away, Steve, the department chair, had forwarded a teaching application fellowship to Virginia. Somehow, Naureen got wind of it, and tried to insist that she, being more senior, should edit the proposal. She went so far as to telephone Virginia and announce, "I want you to forward the fellowship application to me. I won't stand for your advocating teaching approaches I don't approve of."

Virginia was thunderstruck. "Does that mean you plan to censor my pedagogical research?"

Naureen replied with a firm "Yes."

Virginia's righteous indignation flared. "I'm sorry, but there is such a thing as academic freedom, and I can't agree to having my research censored by anyone."

Naureen hung up in a rage. Later, Virginia learned that Naureen tried to get Steve to send her the proposal, but he refused to do so without Virginia's permission.

After that hassle, things got worse. Virginia was awarded the fellowship and used the money to work on some pedagogical innovations, trying to get away from the lecture-memorization-exam-paper model, which, of course, Naureen swore by. Now her courses featured the use of groups, more critical thinking, and less memorization. She still gave exams, but students were expected to apply their knowledge, not list a bunch of rote-learned garbage. The exams were more challenging for her to write, but they were also far more interesting to read than the mushy thinking she'd slogged through in the past.

With the exception of whiners like T.J. and Jason, students loved what Virginia was doing. The trouble was, the more they expressed their approval of Virginia's courses, the more they complained about Naureen. Naureen's response to the pressure was to do everything she could to get rid of Virginia.

Meanwhile, Virginia's success in the classroom was noticed. Steve even asked her to rewrite a course description for the course bulletin—something Naureen had been putting off for years. Virginia's success in the course would finally be codified in the college's most public document. Virginia accepted the assignment and started working on a draft.

Naureen was livid. She saw the issue as an assault on her seniority, not to mention her teaching methods. At last year's promotion hearing, Naureen cannily argued against Virginia's application. Despite strong support from student evaluations and the department chair, the Personnel Committee refused her promotion, though they did renew her contract.

Later, Virginia thought she understood the politics of that decision. The Personnel Committee was composed of senior faculty who understood well the rules of power politics. The foremost rule was: We're doing everything right. There's no need to change. Many of them could identify with Naureen's resistance to pedagogical change, because they were feeling the same pressures in their own departments. They too felt threatened.

When the year finally ended, Virginia felt like she'd been in combat for nine months. Over the summer, she decided to reapply for promotion, reasoning that if she were up for tenure without promotion, Naureen would use her lack of promotion as an excuse for denying tenure. She was in a pickle. There was nothing to do but fight back.

Now she had at least two noisy students who might erode the strong case built by her course evaluations. Not only that, but Steve, who still supported her, kept bugging her for the revised course description that caused so much trouble last year. She wanted to please Steve, but wondered if he realized how nasty Naureen would be when the new description circulated for comments. Would this issue and a couple of disgruntled students spark success for Naureen again?

And where the heck was that exam? Did T.J. actually take it? What if T.J. went to Steve and complained that Virginia lost his exam and wouldn't admit it? T.J. was perfectly capable of bringing an army of friends to vouch for him. Phooey.

Virginia turned off her desk lamp and put her head down on her folded arms. "Time to think, old girl. How can you get yourself out of this pickle?"

# Too Much Thinking

*by Richard Jewell*
University of Minnesota-Twin Cities

## ABSTRACT

This composite of several real-life students and teachers examines Janice, a single mother who has done well in practical courses, and Dr. Terrence, her professor in a critical writing and thinking course. Janice wants to withdraw because she finds the course too difficult. Dr. Terrence is concerned about whether Janice is capable of abstract thought and, if she is, what role he should play in helping her.

## POSSIBLE DISCUSSION QUESTIONS

1. Judging from the material presented in the case, would you say that Janice is qualified to be in Dr. Terrence's course? Why or why not?

2. How would you assess Dr. Terrence's approach to Janice? Would you advise him to change his approach in any way? If so, how?

3. Dr. Terrence researches Janice and her academic work with at least one colleague and the registrar. Is this research appropriate? Should he tell Janice that he will be asking questions of others?

4. Have you encountered students with the problems Janice presents? How have you worked with them? What advice do you have for Dr. Terrence as the clock ticks toward the withdrawal deadline?

# Too Much Thinking

As soon as Janice appeared unannounced at Dr. Terrence's office door at mid-quarter, he realized she was troubled. Her face was rigid with that blank expression students wear when they are controlling negative emotions, and her voice was soft and hesitant as she greeted him. She hovered just inside the door.

His first thought was that a problem had occurred at home: Janice had mentioned previously that she was a single mother with three kids, worked full time at Target, and attended school half time. Her goal was to earn a four-year college degree in the health sciences. Perhaps, he thought, one of her kids had an ear infection, and Janice needed to skip a class to go to the doctor.

"Come on in and sit down," he told her.

She remained standing. "I have to withdraw. I brought the form with me. Here."

"Withdraw from school?" he asked, bewildered.

"Just your class." She was in his Composition 11 course, a required course which offered research writing, reading, and critical thinking. "I'm kind of in a hurry," she said.

"Here," he said, pulling up a chair. "I'll be glad to sign it, but it would help me to hear your reasons why."

Reluctantly she sat, her old wool coat smelling slightly of cigarette smoke. She held on tightly to her inexpensive but clean canvas book bag.

"What's the problem?" he asked.

"I don't know." She shrugged. "I guess it's all this experimental stuff. I'm more used to traditional lectures."

"What is it you don't like?" he asked. "The group work? The writing games?"

"That's part of it," she said.

"You know you don't have to attend every single class," he reminded her, "as long as you replace the missed time with extra writing."

"That would be worse," she exclaimed, "especially if I have to write any more of those critical thinking papers!"

Ah, he thought. The research writing class in their college required students not just to research but also to think. The course met the state system's requirements for critical thinking competencies. Their college taught students how to read arguments and be able to summarize them, react to them, evaluate their quality, and create a research argument. He always explained this in critical thinking terms to his students. His own system for teaching the course was to assign four papers: a summary, a reaction, an evaluation, and a research argument.

"You received a high C on the first paper, the summary," he reminded her." That was not an easy paper."

"Yes," she answered. Then she averted her eyes. "And I got an F on the reaction paper. I've never gotten an F on a paper before." And she started to cry.

He pulled out his box of Kleenex tissues which he kept for such occasions and offered them to her. She took one tissue and wiped her eyes. He was not a tough grader in his department, only average, or at least he was average once the students had used the opportunities he offered for revising their first grades. However, when someone cried, he still felt guilty.

"I'll be glad to give you pointers for revising it," he suggested. "You can raise the grade to a C."

"I'm just so sick and tired of trying to think," she said quickly, dabbing her eyes again. "In the first writing course, all you had to do was write about things that happened to you and why they're important. Now I'm supposed to see a bunch of sides and go outside my own thoughts and see other people's feelings, but how can anybody go into other people's heads or emotions?"

"Do you have your reaction paper with you?" he asked.

"Yes." She pulled it out, handed it to him, and blew her nose as he looked at the paper.

"You did well with your use of quotations. I also like the examples you added from your own experiences," he said. "You spell well, too."

"Thanks." Her voice trembled. "I use spell check."

"Good," he said gently. "You do have some problems with grammar usage and punctuation, but I or a tutor can help you with those. Your main problem is that you summarized your subject instead of reacting to it. You wrote a factual report, but what you need is to argue."

"See what I mean?" she exclaimed, throwing one hand up. "And the next assignment is that stupid evaluation thing, and I don't even understand it! It's just too much thinking." Her tears began flowing again.

Even without seeing her tears, he felt unable to reach a decision. He decided to speak with her previous composition teacher first and then check her academic record.

"Tell you what," he suggested. "How about if we talk more tomorrow? That way you can calm down, and maybe I can come up with some ideas. Okay?"

She nodded and dabbed at her eyes again. "I'm sorry," she said.

"I'll see you tomorrow," he said.

Once she was gone, he picked up his phone. He had always felt that one of the pleasant elements of working at a small college was that teachers were better acquainted with students and could take the time to help them. He hoped his colleague who had taught Janice in Composition might know something more.

"I remember Janice," his colleague told him. "A low-income single mother. I carried her unofficially for the first three weeks of class until her student loan came through. So, I understand, did a couple of other teachers."

"How did she perform academically?"

"In my class? Not that well—a C. Let me find her record. Here it is. Janice wrote an excellent paper from her personal experience and a very good paper giving directions for a process, but she couldn't seem to understand the assignment when the class examined a short story. Her analysis of it was poor. She seemed to have difficulty understanding how to pick a theme and argue it. I'm worried, in fact, that I may have helped her a little too much in developing her theme. But she's very practical. She wrote down every detail of my lectures, made extensive notes in her textbook and reader, and memorized terms well. I thought she deserved at least a C."

Dr. Terrence thanked her, then called the registrar and asked for a quick summary of Janice's record. According to the registrar, Janice had taken developmental courses in reading, math, and writing, and she had passed the reading courses with A and B. However, she was barely working her way through all three of the developmental math courses, with C's in the first two. In developmental writing she had received a B.

Janice did have A's in physical education and the arts and A's and B's in the hard sciences labs, and nursing. But in other courses such as sociology, history, and one philosophy course, she had C's, a D, and several withdrawals. "In fact," the registrar told him, "she's received so many withdrawals that I believe her student loan is in danger of being canceled if she takes any more."

He sighed, sat back in his chair, and wondered what he could tell Janice. She was attentive and studious, but clearly she had trouble with abstract thought. Was she, he wondered, even capable of getting a degree? On the other hand, if she were indeed able to learn better thinking skills, whose responsibility was it? Was it his because the research writing course was one of the few official critical thinking courses on campus? Or did she need more help than he could give her? And of course there was the possibility that she might have to drop college entirely if she had one more withdrawal.

Just then he heard a knock on his door. He looked up, and there was Janice standing in his doorway, grasping her canvas book bag.

"I'm sorry to be such a pain, Dr. Terrence," she said. "But I just found out that the last date to take a passing withdrawal is today." Her eyes began to fill.

She held the form out. "Could you," she asked, "sign it for me now?"

# Grade Expectations

*by Jeannine L. Saabye*
University of Mary

## ABSTRACT

A professor with rigorous standards feels lonely and threatened when a dissatisfied student marshalls other students to complain about the professor's grading system. Issues of standards, student preparation, teacher-student expectations, and faculty accountability all mix together in this case.

## POSSIBLE DISCUSSION QUESTIONS

1. Alice, the student, claims that Kate, the professor, has "changed the rules" by looking for performance on a test that goes beyond rote mastery of the lecture and text material. Does Alice have a point? Why or why not?

2. From the information presented in the case, how do you think Kate prepared the class for the exam? If you were using a similar kind of exam, how would you advise students to prepare?

3. What do you make of Kate's position in her department? Is she respected? If so, why? If not, why not? How does she view her colleagues?

4. What advice would you give Kate and Tom, the department chair, as they plan their encounter tomorrow morning?

# Grade Expectations

Professor Kate Klemmetz pulled her chair up to her desk and started to finger through her inter-campus memos, looking for some real mail. The morning had gone well, she thought, in spite of the fact that she had returned a set of tests to her advanced public speaking course. On the whole, the grades had not been all that good.

"Hey, Kate, why don't you walk down the hall with me to get a cup of coffee?" It was Don Phillips, whose office was next to hers.

"Okay," Kate replied. "I just want to finish looking through this stack of mail."

"You don't sound very enthusiastic."

"Well, I am, actually, but I think I'm still trying to recover from a set of tests I just returned. The level of performance was really pretty poor. Very few A's—lots of C's and D's."

"You're not into giving A's anyway, are you? I thought you were the one with the tough grade reputation," Don joked—though he knew it wasn't a joke. Kate gave fewer A's than anyone else in the department. In fact, her low grade reputation extended well beyond the department's perimeters.

"An A is supposed to mean superior work. I give A's for superior work and am always ready to help any student achieve that."

"Okay, okay. You don't have to get so touchy. Look, I'm starting down the hall; come and join me when you're through at your desk."

"Okay." Kate listened to Don's footsteps slap down the tiled hall. He was a nice guy, but certainly didn't expect much from his students. He never collected written work and was famous for his multiple-choice exams that were recycled from semester to semester. How dare he twit her for requiring more from her students!

Kate sifted through the rest of the mail. Then she switched off the desk lamp, pushed back her chair, picked up her mug, and turned to the door.

Alice was there with her test in her hand.

"Dr. Klemmetz, could I please see you for a few minutes?" Kate put her coffee mug back on her desk. "Is it really important, Alice, or could you come back during my regular office hours in thirty minutes?"

"Well, I can't come back because I have to pick up my daughter at daycare. This is really the only time I have."

"Okay," Kate said, as she sank back into her chair. "Shoot."

"Well, it's about this test. I only got a C and I studied really hard. I even took my daughter over to my sister's two evenings so that I could get enough time to study without interruptions. I knew all the material from the book, and I memorized all my notes from your lectures. Still, all I got was a C."

"You're really frustrated with this grade, aren't you?"

"It just doesn't seem fair that I should get a C when I studied so hard, and I knew all the information. This is the first C that I've gotten since I came back to school. Why, I've been on the Dean's List for two semesters now."

"Well, let's take a look at what went wrong. Maybe next time you'll be able to do better and reach that A you want so badly. Pull up a chair, Alice."

Alice moved the chair closer to the big oak desk. She put her book bag on the floor, then opened her test to the first page. The specifics of Alice's test started to come back to Kate.

"Alice, if you recall the discussion we had in class, I think you will remember I said that it would be important to use correct spelling and grammar on the test. You lost some points on each question for little mechanical errors."

"I'm working on this stuff. In fact, I go to the Learning Center for extra help on grammar and punctuation, and my tutor says it's getting better. I guess a person doesn't get credit for trying."

"In the long run, you'll definitely benefit from your efforts, but I think you'd have to agree that your work on this test isn't yet up to standards."

Alice narrowed her eyes and set her jaw. "Well, I thought this was a public speaking course, not a public writing course."

Kate could feel her neck turn red, but she did not raise her voice. With a few deep breaths, she nipped the urge to lash out.

"I'm sure you wonder why I give so much weight to writing. It's important for you to hone your skills in a host of areas if you plan to graduate and be able to perform at a basic professional level." Alice looked down, but said nothing.

"But really, Alice, you know that punctuation and grammar alone didn't bring your grade down to a C. Do you know what did?"

"Well, I know what you said in class, but—"

Kate interrupted, "You said it yourself: you gave back all the information from the text and my lectures, word for word, but that doesn't show me that you understand the concepts. Even your examples are the ones I gave you."

Kate could see Alice's anger start to rise, but she continued. "You see? Take a look at question 6, for instance. It gives you eight examples of logical fallacies, asks you to identify the fallacy at work and to explain, in your own words, why you think so. In your own words, not the book's. Question 4 asks you to give examples from your own experience. You gave examples from the lectures. It's not enough for you to parrot back what you read in the book or heard in a lecture."

"How can it not be enough? It's always been enough! I've been on the Dean's List two semesters. I'm not this dumb. You're the one who's changing the rules—teaching us to learn from your high and mighty lectures and this fifty-dollar book—and then testing us on something else! It's not fair! And I'm not a C student!" Alice's anger filled the room.

Quietly, Kate said, "There is nothing wrong with a C, which means average work. To get an A or a B, you must be able to do these other things. I would be perfectly willing to work with you, or we can arrange for a tutor. We will also work more on thinking skills in class, which should help you improve on the next exam."

"I need an A now. Can't I do some extra credit to bring this test grade up?"

"I'm sorry, but this test is finished. Let's concentrate on the future and your continued improvement."

"I understand that the test is finished, but I still think you tested us on stuff that was too different from what we did in class. I just don't get it—how can I know the material cold but get a C?"

"Alice, I don't think you know the material at all. You know how to repeat what you've been told or what you've read in a book, but this test proves that you can't apply that knowledge."

"I think you're being unfair. Others think so too. You change the rules, like I said before. No wonder you hardly ever give good grades."

"I don't give any grades, Alice. Anyone can earn an A in my class if they are willing to work hard enough to reach true excellence. I'm sorry you're disappointed in your grade, but I can't change it."

"Then I'm going to talk to someone else about this. I was the only one who had the nerve to come talk to you, but plenty of others are unhappy about your grading system too! A whole lot of others!"

Kate didn't move. She didn't say any more. She let Alice stomp out and she listened to the echo of her heels down the hall. She was certain that Alice would go to the department chair, if not the dean. She wasn't sure how many students would support Alice. What was the level of discontent in her class?

---

By the end of the afternoon, Tom Stockton, the department chair, was at her door. Eight students from the twenty-five member class had been in his office complaining about her grading policies. It wasn't the first time he'd heard students out, but this group seemed angrier than others—or was he intimidated by their numbers, in spite of himself? And why did they have to barge in just before lunch? Thanks to the confrontation, he had terrible heartburn. What was Kate trying to prove? And why did he have to defend her at the expense of his health?

Tom assumed Kate would be defensive, so he tried to ignore his stomach and keep things light. "I don't want to interfere in your class, and I certainly don't want to tell you how to teach or how to grade, but maybe it's time to rethink things a little bit, Kate."

"My standards are not unreasonable."

"No, they probably aren't. You have high expectations for your students, but maybe you need to rethink things. This is the third time in as many semesters that I've fielded complaints about your grading policies. I don't want any more. Do something."

Kate was stunned. What was she supposed to do? It wasn't her problem. Poorly prepared students were the problem. Students who thought memorizing was learning were the problem. Not to mention other lax faculty who encouraged that delusion—people like her colleague Don, who gave undeserved A's and B's. It was no secret in the department that Don—and others—had lowered their expectations and, when they thought they had to, granted A's and B's to avoid confrontation. She would never stoop to that. Her students would earn their A's for creative, critical thinking, and they would be proud of those A's when they got them.

Tom knew the script. He was prepared to listen to Kate lament the decline of academic standards and their colleagues' corresponding lack of responsibility. In part, he knew she was right, but he was tired of conflict. And his stomach hurt.

Before she could gather herself to respond, Tom announced, "I'd like you to come in and discuss this situation with me tomorrow morning. Nine o'clock okay? A plan about some modification in your approach would be good. The students can't be all wrong—not a third of the class. You know I've defended you endless times in the past. It isn't that you don't have a point. But you ought to be thinking about your course evaluations as well as your sacred standards. You just can't hang on that tightly, Kate. Give in a little, for God's sake." Tom tried to soften his tone with a smile, but feared it looked more like a wince.

After a long pause, Kate said, "Nine o'clock will be fine."

# The Jonas Incident

*by Chris M. Anson*
University of Minnesota-Twin Cities

## ABSTRACT

Writing teachers are used to seeing papers develop rhetorically and stylistically as students become more practiced in the writing process. In this case, a student submits a paper that is well written according to objective criteria, even though the writer did not revise between drafts. However, the content wars with the instructor's values and makes assessment an ideological rather than a rhetorical act.

## POSSIBLE DISCUSSION QUESTIONS

1. Is Cynthia's course of action (relying on her revision policy to determine Jonas' grade) appropriate? Why or why not?

2. Does Jonas have a right to express his views, even if some might consider them racist? Does Cynthia have a right to "ban" certain ideas or expression from her class?

3. If a small group, like the one Jonas is in, agrees with a writer's views and encourages little revision, is the writer justified in assuming the paper needs little further conceptual work or revision? Why or why not?

4. Respond to the following parts of a dialogue about this case:

Ed: "I think Cynthia is out of line here. She's reacting personally to Jonas' ideas and not to what she's teaching, which is good writing."

Sue: "I agree. Writing teachers have a responsibility to make good writers, not good liberals or good conservatives. If I were Cynthia, my duty would be to make Jonas the best racist writer I could, by finding better support for his arguments."

Paula: "No, I think as teachers we have a moral obligation to help students to be fair people and good citizens. I'm not sure I agree with Cynthia's tactics, but I sure do agree with her that Jonas needs to learn about his racism."

Sam: "How can you call him racist? He's simply pointing out a problem in the black community—and doing it pretty well at that. I almost agree with him!"

# The Jonas Incident

"Well, you say all this stuff about linking ideas," Jonas Simmons almost shouted, "but what's really behind this is that you just don't like my position. And I'm probably the last honest student in this class."

The rest of the class had already left the room, but Cynthia was nevertheless embarrassed by Jonas' words, uttered in a kind of clenched-teeth bitterness that made her almost afraid to respond. And his confrontation was all the more disconcerting because he had never given Cynthia any reason to believe he would challenge her so forcefully. An articulate student, Jonas had written his first paper in Cynthia's Introduction to Sociology course on the psycho-social response to highway entrance-ramp stoplights; using some statistics he had gathered from the highway department, as well as observations and interviews with drivers, he had argued convincingly that the lights had led to alternative behaviors that did little to alleviate the problem of traffic jams and resulted in more aggressive driving. But in spite of his abilities, Jonas had also been very withdrawn during class sessions, often joining groups reluctantly, waiting for others to volunteer to discuss their ideas. In discussions, he would usually keep silent, but occasionally come forward with a short, carefully worded statement. There was also something just a little off-center about his demeanor, Cynthia had thought—he made odd, subtle facial expressions from time to time as she or other students talked.

As she had gotten to know the class over the past few weeks of the term, Cynthia weighed her comments on Jonas' work carefully, finding herself sometimes torn between thinking her cautiousness was a sell-out for not being more confrontational about his sometimes odd ideas, and worrying that something—what, she had no idea—could come from pushing too hard at this rather unusual student.

In her three years of teaching at Pound Ridge University, Cynthia had not encountered any students who had presented problems for her. A generally successful teacher, she taught her classes in what some of her peers felt was a pretty standard way, focusing on the learning of the subject, helping students to develop their ideas and find support or evidence for assertions, and allowing students some freedom to choose topics to explore in their papers. In her committee work and in departmental meetings, she had become more outspoken since her first year, often challenging people's ideas but never abrasively. Now she felt a growing desire to do the same thing in her sociology classes.

For the second assignment in her course, Cynthia had asked the class to choose a recent event that could be understood through the lens of the sociological concepts the class was studying, and then write a commentary on the event from a sociological perspective. Her assignment sheet stressed the need to be "thoughtful," and not to rely on sound bites from the media. In her example, she alluded to the Bobbit "assault." "What's at stake, sociologically speaking?" she asked rhetorically. "What issues does this event raise about the concept of abuse? Was Bobbit right, based on the evidence? What is justifiable revenge in our society? How can we link this event to sociological concepts and theories?"

In this second assignment, Cynthia formed the students into small groups to give each other some feedback on their rough drafts. Pressured by an overdue book review for an academic journal, she did not have the time to write up a revision guide with questions that would focus the students' attention on important issues in their papers. Instead, she suggested some things to look for, then set the students to work. She noticed that Jonas was, as usual, the last to join his group, reluctantly moving his chair over and sitting with his peers, three other young men whom Cynthia felt she didn't know very well yet. She noticed that toward the end of the session, with about five minutes to spare, the group began talking about Jonas' paper, but she was busy with another group and didn't hear any of what they said.

At the end of the unit, as Cynthia sat in her office reading papers, she was generally impressed with the quality of students' work. When she reached Jonas' paper, her feelings about his abilities were confirmed—his opening, which used a personal anecdote, was well written and appealing. But as she continued to read, she felt herself bristling, shaking her head, and then boiling with anger. Jonas had written a paper more blatantly racist than anything she had ever seen as a faculty member. She sat, stunned, looking at his work.

### Thieving, the Black Community, and Fragmented Values

*Jonas Simmons*

When I was young, about six or seven, I stole my cousin's harmonica. It was a beautiful instrument given to him as a gift, silver with gold inlay. Finding myself in his room alone, I slipped it into my pocket in a moment of sudden insanity, and left his house.

The values inculcated in my household were strong enough that for days I wrestled with the guilt of my theft. Peter didn't miss the harmonica; his family was wealthy, and we were on the poor side of middle-class; he had a multitude of toys, games, and recreational opportunities. Maybe he thought he had just misplaced it, and went off to do something else. I'm not sure. Still, these possibilities didn't console me at all. After a time, during which the harmonica sat idle in the bottom drawer of my dresser (which opened with a special knack only I possessed), I decided to return it. I couldn't play it without being heard, and showing it to anyone would have revealed my theft.

But unlike the theft, this time the deceit wasn't so easy. For one thing, it didn't carry the same heart-pounding, terrible glee. It was also harder. I needed a reason to see my cousin, I didn't want to wait until an invitation came along months later, and I needed an opportunity that might never come again—a chance to be alone again in Peter's room. Of course, there was also simple confession, but the idea soon took on an awful complexity that made the subterfuge tidy by comparison, an equal and opposite reaction that would wipe out all traces of my lapse from grace.

The plan eventually worked, and the details are now unimportant in the scope of my claim. Of relevance here is the magnitude of this event in my memory and my growth. But why was it so important? Not because of "me" in an essentialist way, but because of the values instilled in me by my parents and community.

Now imagine a young black teenager shortly after the first Rodney King verdict was announced by the press. Caught in a tide of hatred and hostility, he joins a small band of his friends and goes on a tirade of looting and destruction in his community. Why is it that this kid, hardly man enough to shave (if he cared at all about his appearance), would turn against his own kind and rob them, destroying their property while taking pleasure in his actions? The reasons are obvious. His race, once struggling to pass on deeply felt values through its generations, has lost the vision of its own morality. Black mothers in the inner city are often more worried about getting the next dose of crack than raising their kids to become decent citizens. Black men give the youngsters in their community the role model of thugs, thieves, addicts, and pimps. More impassioned by the desire for sleek cars and CD players than the concept of guiding the younger generation toward health of spirit, they begin to care only for themselves and their own conditions. How many looters after the riots really felt even a twinge of regret? How many even considered taking back their stolen boom boxes, TVs, or leather coats? (Even if they had, their sin had already done their cousins in; the stores remained closed, battered and boarded in the desolate streets of the Los Angeles ghettos.)

There may be no solution, at least immediate, to this inner-city moral blight. Liberals always blame the system for creating the conditions that lead to such lapses in the black culture's moral center. But history has shown examples again and again of people in the most abject circumstances rising above their degradation by the energy of moral spirit. Where has it gone? The historian Thomas Holt, in an essay tracing the black struggle for literacy, notes the same loss of values in the black community, only this time toward education. Cut from the same cloth, the urge for learning and morality has largely disappeared from a majority of black "households," replaced by guns, drugs, open sexuality, vulgarity, child abuse, battered women, and a shunning of physical health and well-being.

Liberals make members of the "dominant culture," the "hegemony," keep blaming themselves and bailing out inner-city blacks for their own communities' loss of a moral center. But this solution does nothing to create changes within. More sensible is a strong message to these communities: no pain, no gain. No focus by black people on their own problems, no regaining of the moral center. And no more bailouts.

While some critics may argue that the needs of poor communities make them unable to do "grander" things, I would argue the opposite. Morality transcends even hunger. Can I help those communities? I used to think it was my obligation. Now I wash my conscience of them. They must help themselves, and show the rest of society that they are worthy of the dignity they once deserved.

While reading Jonas' paper, Cynthia wrote no comments on it, feeling almost as if it were like a dangerous virus. Then, very deliberately, she opened up her word-processor and typed out the following note:

Jonas: I'm afraid I must return your essay without grading it. As you know, I have strong feelings about a number of issues, especially racism, which your paper only promotes. Since I can't judge your essay fairly, I won't judge it at all. Because the issue here is ideological, I will ask that you write another paper on a different topic, and I will give you the rest of the term to do so. Please submit a rough draft to me at least two weeks before the end of the term, so you can revise it for final submission.

> I will apply the grade on the revised paper to your average. If you
> choose not to do this, you will receive no credit for this unit.

As soon as she typed in the last word of her note, Cynthia had misgivings about this strategy. Although she had no reason to think that Jonas wouldn't just go off and write a new paper, something about the refusal to grade his work kept nagging at her. She had talked with other teachers who had done this before, but always in connection with the "quality" of their writing (and for their own good!). But not for their ideas. But, she mused—weren't ideas also quality? Furthermore, these teachers had always returned the papers after the students had worked on a draft. Now here was Jonas, having benefited from his group's comments, turning in a paper that was not very different from the original. In fact, it was hardly revised. Still, Cynthia felt apprehensive about a comparative analysis of Jonas' rough and final drafts as the main basis for her grade. A year ago, she wouldn't have given it a second thought: her syllabus had made it clear that the improvement of the writing, based on peer feedback, would weigh heavily in her assessment of each unit. Predictably, many of her students received high grades by virtue of their efforts alone. Several times, her department chair had raised the issue of grade-inflation, urging the faculty to toughen up on their standards. For Cynthia, this had led to some shifts in the way she read papers and told students about her evaluations. Her syllabus now included the following revised statement of her criteria:

> I will expect you to make use of opportunities that our class provides
> you to work on your papers (such as small-group revision sessions). I
> will collect rough and final drafts, but will only judge the quality of the
> final draft, not the extent to which you have improved it. Opportunities
> for revision are yours to use, not mine to grade. Make use of them, and
> your final papers will be better.

Glancing at the comments of Jonas' conference partners, Cynthia regretted abandoning her old improvement criteria; back then, she could have easily given Jonas a D for not having revised it. What else was there? As she scanned her assignment sheet, she suddenly realized that Jonas hadn't referred directly to anything they had been reading in the course. Not one theory, not one concept, was explicitly linked to the event Jonas was describing. A feeling of vindication washing over her, she penned in at the bottom: "This doesn't fully respond to the assignment—D+." She put the paper aside. She would worry about commenting on it later.

---

As if reading her mind, Jonas continued to challenge the basis of Cynthia's grade. "The fact that I don't mention five theories isn't relevant. It's not what these papers are supposed to do, at least by your own admission," he said, looking off toward the window as if addressing something there. "These are my thoughts about a sociological event, and I doubt that you'll find any errors in the writing."

Cynthia knew she couldn't criticize his writing on technical grounds or even, for that matter, stylistically. There was no question that Jonas was as decent a writer, from this perspective, as she'd ever had. She had to rely, then, on something rhetorical, but other than the reference issue, all that came to mind, in an objective way, was audience—Jonas hadn't considered his readers. "See," she started hesitantly, "I think what's missing from your paper is a strong acknowledgment of your audience. I mean, let's face it, lots of people would find this piece pretty blatantly racist." Feeling as if she were becoming trapped, she added hesitantly, "Most sociologists are more objective than this."

"No," Jonas challenged, still looking at the window. "You found it racist. But I imagined an audience of like-minded thinkers. I hear these sentiments expressed on a daily basis, even in this class."

"No, not here, Jonas," Cynthia said firmly. "Not once in this class, and you know it."

"You don't know it," Jonas retorted. "They're just playing the game. You can't know what I know; you're the teacher. That's why they didn't give me anything to change. Besides, most of us aren't even sociology majors."

Cynthia felt herself becoming defensive. "I don't care what they think outside my class," she blurted. "In here, no racism. Period."

Jonas, now looking at her directly for the first time, handed Cynthia his paper. He waited until, with a puzzled look, she took it. "I won't take up the issue of freedom of speech," he said very formally. "I ask only that you reconsider my grade objectively, based on the quality of the writing. I know you'll change your mind." For a second, Cynthia felt that she had never met a more displeasing individual. Then Jonas left the room.

Later that day, wondering whether she should consult a member of the administrative staff, Cynthia checked her mailbox to see if there had been any fallout from the Jonas incident. There was only one thing in her box. It was a copy of an item one of the members of the faculty-development staff had pinned on the bulletin board next to the mailboxes.

Seven Principles of Good Practice in Undergraduate Education
- Good practice encourages student-faculty contact.
- Good practice encourages cooperation among students.
- Good practice encourages active learning.
- Good practice gives prompt feedback.
- Good practice emphasizes time on task.
- Good practice communicates high expectations.
- Good practice respects diverse talents and ways of learning.
    —From the AAHE, Education Commission of the States, and the Johnson
      Foundation

At first, Cynthia thought that perhaps the faculty-development program had decided to give all teachers a copy of the item. Surreptitiously, she pulled out the contents of some of her colleagues' mailboxes to see if the item was there as well; it was not. As she did this, looking around to be sure no one was nearby, she felt a strange sense of confused embarrassment, no doubt coming from a residue of feeling about Jonas' paper. As if caught in a little breach of ethics, she quickly thrust the papers back in her colleagues' box and stared at the copy of the item. Why was this here? Then she noticed a tiny asterisk penned next to the last item on the list.

It had to be Jonas.

# Part III: Cases about Departments and Institutions

# Introduction

*by Carol Rutz*
University of Minnesota-Twin Cities

As professionals, teachers are constantly challenged to meet expectations from their institutions, their peers, their students, and the public. Career teachers can find themselves out of step—or ahead of the curve. New teachers struggle to develop a personal teaching style while completing an initiation process en route to earning full credentials. Teachers who are willing to examine their teaching and reflect on their performance may experience epiphany—or misery.

This section of cases offers a range of situations where teachers must take account of their institutional settings as they do their classroom work. Many of the dynamics of classroom and professional relationships come into play. For instance, "The Academic Purist" features a successful, well-prepared lecturer who resists sharing control of the course material in any way. Can she change her approach? Should she?

In "Best in the Class," a brilliant student writes an anonymous, but identifiable, evaluation of his teaching assistant that accuses her of failing to teach him. Linda, the teacher in training, worries about her supervisor's reaction to the evaluation. She also wants to know what went wrong. Should she confront the student?

External factors often affect curricular and pedagogical directions. "The Fly in the Ointment" deals with a balky senior professor who is unwilling to dance to an accreditation body's tune. Does academic freedom protect fractiousness?

Academic freedom also plays a role in the delicate matter of tenure and promotion. "Risky Business" outlines a particularly complex case where a department chair tries to balance a candidate's innovative teaching performance against student complaints, a hostile senior professor, and new institutional guidelines.

Service on institutional committees can bring faculty into awkward confrontations with one another. As Ashish Kumar learns in "To 'B' or Not to 'B': A Case of Academic Appeal," this kind of clash can be particularly disturbing when one's advice to a colleague results in that colleague's being called on the carpet.

Collaborative projects among faculty enhance research and the curriculum. However, close work among folks of different ranks and departments may reveal unexpected personal beliefs. In "To Tell or Not to Tell," a junior faculty member learns about a senior colleague's politically incorrect views from a student. Institutional commitment to diversity and many other power issues must be sorted out.

Many institutions are tempted to view students as consumers, which puts departments in a marketing role as they recruit faculty and design their curricula. What happens when an "Unpopular Senior Professor" won't play ball? How can a department work with a person who disdains ignorance and uses rigorous standards to scare away students? What effect will he have on recruiting new faculty?

Mentoring programs for junior faculty can be wonderful support systems for new teachers as they work toward tenure. In "Wendy Lamb," a young physics professor with strong teaching evaluations welcomes her mentor's visits to her class—until a number of students drop the course and the remaining students show signs of disinterest. What role should her mentor play?

When faculty are brought together in an interdisciplinary task force on a large project, tensions are inevitable. "Assessment at Woebegone State" shows vividly the difficulties of pleasing everyone involved while dealing with resistance at many levels.

Those who have opportunities to teach abroad relish the exposure to new places and all the cultural wonders that go with them. However, the teaching situation may be less than wonderful. Two exchange teachers compare notes in "Is Something Rotten in Denmark?" and discover that their expectations were unrealistic.

Finally, anyone who dismisses the notion that teaching is political will have to revisit that thinking after reading "Teaching Semantics." In this case, a linguist finds himself accused of using offensive language in class. In trying to demonstrate the emotional power of taboo language, Dr. Fisher is burned by the response—especially when the dean conveys a student complaint.

Institutional contexts vary, but the situations described in these cases have a haunting universal feel to them. Close examination of these conflicts should be fruitful.

# The Academic Purist

*by Deborah Petersen-Perlman*
University of Minnesota-Duluth

## ABSTRACT

This case features the struggle of a classically trained scholar-professor who has come to desire change in her lecture-driven classes. The professor connects with a peer observer to facilitate new directions in her teaching. She finds herself resistant to change, and most particularly, to relinquishing control so as to encourage more active student participation.

## POSSIBLE DISCUSSION QUESTIONS

1. Is there a problem? Jane's student evaluation numbers are high. Students' expectations are being met. Why fix it if it ain't broke?

2. Why do you think Jane is so resistant to trying the suggestions made by her partner?

3. Are there alternative teaching modes beyond Donna's suggestion which might be more comfortable for Jane?

4. How should Donna confront Jane on her unwillingness to try the timeline?

# The Academic Purist

Donna looked to her right. The student sitting next to her was alternately shaking out his writing hand and then massaging it. It took him just a few seconds and then he resumed his note taking at a fast and furious pace. Donna scanned the rest of the classroom. Every single student's head was down, pens to paper, as they desperately struggled to keep up with the teacher. Donna redirected her attention to the front of the classroom and took note of the time. Jane, the professor, had been lecturing at a comfortable pace for an hour already; her lecture style was fluid and nonstop.

Donna briefly reviewed her notes. There had been only one question from the students during the entire class period, and that query had merely asked for repetition of an important date. Jane had paused twice to solicit student response to questions she had posed, and both times the same student (sitting in row two of a large classroom) offered the correct answer. Other than that, Jane had held forth blithely demonstrating her impressive mastery of the subject matter. Jane referred to the assigned texts for the class as well as her own extensive research on the topic for the day. At various points, Jane took issue with the authors of the assigned texts, thereby identifying her own thoughtful interpretations of the events she was discussing.

Nobody can fault her for her preparation, Donna thought, but what a marathon session this had been. She reflected on her recent meeting with Jane.

Jane and Donna were colleagues in the College of Liberal Arts. Upon hearing about a college-sponsored peer observation program, the two women decided to form a partnership. Donna was to visit Jane's class and Jane would return the favor. The visit to Donna's class was scheduled for the following week because Jane had decided she wanted to go first.

At their meeting prior to the observation of Jane's class, Donna asked Jane to describe her goals for the upcoming session.

"I want the students to see the individual events which were taking place during this period within the larger framework of the twentieth century," Jane replied. She continued, "I have asked them to read three books and I expect them to attend lecture faithfully. I just hope they will be ready for my presentation of this material."

"What would you like me to take note of when I'm in the classroom?" Donna asked.

"I'm concerned that the students may not be 'getting it' all the time. I really don't know if they see all of the intricate connections I am trying to make for them. Sometimes I feel as though I am talking at them instead of making a connection."

Donna picked up on Jane's implication that interaction between students and teacher might be nonexistent, so she offered a suggestion, "Maybe you could try to get the students more physically involved in the lecture. Instead of your taking full responsibility for the timeline, could you draw a continuum on the board, and at different points during the class period maybe you could invite students up to the board to fill in key events and actors in those events?"

"But that will take a great deal of time, and I have a lot of material I need to cover in order to prepare them for their midterm examination," Jane protested.

"Well...," Donna paused. She could not help but feel Jane's resistance. How to put this, she wondered. "Perhaps you could ask a few volunteers to begin the process just before class is to start. They could get the timeline started by identifying the events and players you've covered so far. Then when it's time for the mid-period break, you could ask a few others to come up and fill in what you have covered during the first half of class."

"I just don't know," Jane interrupted. "I'm concerned that they may make some mistakes. Then I'll have to waste time correcting their errors."

"How much time do you think such corrections would take? Wouldn't the students benefit by trying to contextualize these events themselves rather than having to rely on you?"

The expression on Jane's face had been prophetic. Donna knew before she arrived in the classroom that Jane was not ready to try anything this risky. Sure enough, the class had progressed in the traditional lecture mode.

Donna was concerned about how she and Jane were going to discuss this situation. It seemed to Donna that Jane's participation in the peer observation program was somewhat problematic. Why was she involved? What did she want to get out of the experience? In spite of these questions, Donna knew that Jane was concerned about her teaching; she just wasn't sure about Jane's specific goals.

Donna thought about what she knew of Jane. The two women had spent some time discussing their respective professional identities. Jane's self-image as a teacher was that of a teller. She trained to become the consummate political scientist and she learned from the "best." She emulated her teachers from her Ivy League and Cambridge alma maters. These learned professors professed! She attempted to do likewise.

Jane told Donna that she loved her subject with a passion; she immersed herself in it completely. When she related stories to Donna based on her various research trips to Russia and other Eastern European nations, she spoke in reverent, almost hushed tones. She believed that what she had to say offered a unique perspective unavailable in books or articles. There was so much to say, she said, that she felt constrained by the limits of each class period. Donna got the impression that each word Jane uttered was carefully chosen, like a precious pearl which the students treasured and examined in careful detail.

Donna knew that students dared not miss too many classes, because if they did, they would fall behind hopelessly. The books and articles Jane assigned were supplementary to these fact-packed lectures. Every class session was exhausting for both Jane and the class.

Even though Jane's students' test results usually formed a bell curve and her student evaluations were well above normal, she told Donna that she felt that something was missing, and therefore she felt dissatisfied. Obviously, an hour and forty minutes, twice a week, was not sufficient to convey all of the information she believed was so important to her students' knowledge base. Jane confessed that she knew the five or ten students who regularly contributed answers to the questions she posed, but there were an additional fifty or sixty who remained anonymous to her. These students came to class, Jane said, but they never participated in class or visited during office hours. Donna's perception was that her contact with them remained mostly unidirectional. She admitted to Donna that part of what she felt was missing was a lack of student enthusiasm for the subject. Yes, they listened; yes, they acknowledged her mastery of the subject, but they did not return her passion for this endlessly fascinating material. Jane pondered out loud how to make her love for her topic contagious. Donna knew that the real question was "What could she do to involve her students more deeply in the course without imposing more of a burden on herself than what already existed?"

From Jane's point of view, the practice of almost straight lecture always seemed well-suited to the traditional political science class. It was Donna's sense that Jane believed that she dared not veer too far away from this "I talk, you listen" mode, or she would not complete all of the valuable material she felt she needed to convey. Donna knew that, ultimately, Jane always wanted to be in control of this classroom.

After her observation of Jane's class, Donna sat down and massaged her temples. The class had indeed been an intellectual workout and she felt worn out. She reflected on her experiences with some anxiety. Their post-observation meeting was scheduled for the next day and Donna was not sure where to begin their discussion. Donna felt as though she should address Jane's unwillingness to experiment with new techniques to engage the students, but she also knew there were a number of other, more fundamental questions which she wanted Jane to answer. Donna kept coming back to one of her original concerns: What did Jane want to get out of this peer observation program?

# Best in the Class

*by Carol Rutz*
University of Minnesota-Twin Cities

## ABSTRACT

What happens when an outstanding student participates fully in a writing class, writes exceptionally well, and claims to be dissatisfied? In this case, the teacher and student have radically different views of the course: The teacher is thrilled with the student's work; the student's course-evaluation comments may doom the teacher's future teaching assignment.

## POSSIBLE DISCUSSION QUESTIONS

1. What are the teaching issues at work in this case?

2. How could Linda have learned more about Brian (and the other students) in order to head off some misunderstanding?

3. Should Brian have been exempt from this course?

4. If exemption or placement in an honors section were not possibilities, how could Linda have challenged him more effectively?

5. At the end of the case, Linda fears two confrontations: one with Brian, the other with her supervisor. What advice do you have for her as she deals with each person?

# Best in the Class

Linda was flattered and a little nervous about being assigned a course called "writing about science." As an English graduate teaching assistant, she had an undergraduate transcript with minimal traces of formal science. This course was far outside her usual range. Therefore, Linda prepared herself to take a kindly view of the passive voice and to concentrate on the IMRAD form (introduction, methods and materials, results, and discussion), a staple of published scientific discourse. However, she was surprised to learn that the course description specified writing about science for broader audiences. Rather than teaching students how to prepare data for scientific publications, her task was to help them learn to interpret science to lay audiences that might include granting agencies, scientists outside one's individual specialty, corporate supervisors, and even readers of newspapers and popular magazines.

With considerable apprehension, Linda prepared her syllabus, knowing that this course was being offered to her on a probationary basis. Could she keep up with the students? Linda reasoned that assignments dealing with critical analysis of published research would give students a decent challenge, especially when combined with a longer project geared toward a popular audience.

On the first day of class, Linda asked the students to introduce themselves and tell, among other things, their expectations of the course. Because admission to the course was controlled, all of the students were majoring in some sort of science or engineering. Most of them were planning to graduate at the end of the current (spring) quarter. Linda then walked them through the syllabus, emphasizing the kind of writing that they would be doing. Some students were relieved that they were not expected to write "professional" scientific prose. Others were clearly disappointed about not writing the kind of formal research papers that they wanted to practice. For some of them, this was their last chance to hone skills that they wanted polished for graduate and professional school.

One person in the latter camp was Brian, a physics major, who mentioned that one of his expectations was to work on a paper he expected to publish during the coming summer. Linda was not too worried about disappointing Brian because she knew that her assignments would still give him many opportunities to improve his writing. She made a mental note to keep his personal goals in mind as the term progressed.

Brian's concerns came out more forcefully at the end of the first week of class. Two of Linda's colleagues observed the class and participated with the students as they collaborated on the format they would use to critique scientific journal articles. Brian happened to sit at the visitors' table and voiced his frustration with the assignment to them and the others in their small group. Why use a critical approach that essentially interpreted scientific findings for an audience that would never read those findings as they were published? Why not rely on the published data and look at the tables and figures that speak for themselves? Why "dumb down" the material? Complex scientific research demands sophisticated language and presentation. To Brian, the assignment seemed disrespectful of the material.

Linda's colleagues shared Brian's objections with her, as well as their attempts to persuade him of the worthiness of Linda's assignments. Brian's intensity gave them pause; would this student derail Linda's class? They reminded Linda that their supervisor read student evaluations closely and used those evaluations to make decisions on teaching assignments. Given her inexperience, even one articulate student with an axe to grind could prevent Linda from being assigned any writing courses next year. This course was probationary, after all. How would she stay in graduate school without a teaching job?

Linda still wasn't too worried. Student evaluations were many weeks away. Besides, she did not think Brian would be vindictive, even if the course were not exactly what he wanted. She saw Brian as a bright person who would see the point eventually. Once he did one or two of the assignments and read what others wrote, he would be fine.

As Brian and the rest of the class worked on their critiques, they exchanged drafts with one another. Coming from many different majors, most students had to give feedback about topics that they did not know well. As they asked questions of one another, all of them, including Brian, began to appreciate the need to communicate clearly even with a highly literate scientific population, such as the members of the class. No one is an expert in everything, after all.

Once he accepted the nature of the writing assignments, Brian's work was exemplary. He spent a great deal of time on his papers, writing many extra drafts that showed thoughtful, self-reflexive revision. On the second paper, Linda found herself writing, "You obviously know what you are doing, Brian. I will push you to be as clear as possible in these critiques, since your understanding of the material is so sophisticated. You have a good sense of structure, tone, and diction. Let me know if you have specific writing questions you would like me to advise you on."

After midterm, Linda held individual conferences with all of the students to talk about a longer paper. Brian had submitted a draft that, for him, was atypical—rather short and superficial. Linda assumed that he had been preoccupied with midterm exams and other assignments. She knew he would attend the scheduled conference to tell her his plans for this paper.

Brian came to her office a couple of minutes late. "Hi," he said, seating himself and rummaging in his book bag. "Sorry I'm late."

"No problem," smiled Linda. "We have plenty of time. Tell me what you plan to do with this paper—I'm assuming that you haven't had much time to work on it."

Brian blushed. "It's a mess. I'm really ashamed to hand in anything so sketchy. But I had two horrible midterms that conflicted with this draft—plus the research I'm working on has taken a heckuva lot of time these last few weeks. I'm planning, though, to set aside some more time for this—I want to do a really thorough job. Here's what I'm going to do."

Brian then outlined an ambitious approach that far exceeded the demands of the assignment. Linda could barely follow him. She shifted in her chair, preparing to interrupt with a question when Brian stopped in mid-sentence and looked right at her.

"The other thing that's driving me nuts is all the planning I have to do. My wife is expecting our first child this summer, and I'm starting a very small and competitive graduate program in the fall. But they really want me to start early, before the baby comes, which would mean relocating as well as finishing up the quarter and closing out my research here...." What started as a rush of emotion trailed off into silence as Brian looked away.

Linda paused. Quietly, she said, "Brian, in light of all this pressure, why don't you take a less ambitious approach to this paper? You are doing excellent work in the course, and I know you can focus more narrowly and still write a fine paper. Believe me,

I look forward to reading it—but I don't want you to drive yourself crazy trying to write something definitive while dealing with the rest of your courses—and your life!"

Brian sighed. He took some notes as Linda made suggestions. They shook hands, and he left, looking preoccupied.

Linda wondered to herself, "Did I offend him? Does he feel patronized rather than encouraged? I wish I had known before today that he's older than the other students and has all of these distractions. The poor guy has so much to handle." But Tina, the next student, was waiting, so Linda shifted her attention to her.

For the rest of the term, Brian continued to participate in class and write well. His final paper was easily the best of a very good bunch. Linda found herself completely absorbed in his argument. She commented on the paper extensively, feeling that she was truly in dialogue with Brian as a writer. She looked forward to chatting with him when he picked his paper up during finals week. Never, she thought, had she worked with such a bright and thoughtful student.

Once grades were in, Linda had time to kill while waiting for students to retrieve their papers. Department policy allowed teaching assistants to review their course evaluations as soon as the grade sheets were submitted, so Linda read over the generally positive comments from her students. One student, however, was quite critical.

Linda recognized Brian's handwriting. He wrote that he did not feel his writing had improved during the courses. In his view, he wrote "pretty well" when he began the class and received little feedback that made much difference in his writing. Furthermore, the course was not what he expected, since he wanted to learn more about science writing. It was possible, he went on, that the assigned papers required more thought and writing agility than conventional scientific writing assignments. Nevertheless, he saw little application to his needs as a scientist except in the sense that practice is always of some value. The course was basically worthless.

Linda was stunned. She sat in her office, wondering what to say to him when he came for his paper. Should she compliment him on the paper? Should she tell him she recognized his handwriting on the evaluation form? Should she tell him that his comments could prevent her from teaching writing next year? Should she ask his advice in dealing with future students like him? Or should she just forget it? Would it be more professional to just wish him well and learn from her mistake? But what was her mistake? She thought anxiously about her supervisor and her probationary status in the department. What had gone wrong? Or was anything wrong? How could she know without talking with Brian? But what could she say?

A knock at the door startled her. Brian pushed the door open a crack.

Linda gestured toward him. "Come in."

# The Fly in the Ointment

*by James Swanson*
Dakota State University

## ABSTRACT

This is a case of a faculty member who invokes the protection of academic freedom to resist the changes and teaching innovations required by his institution's accreditation plan. It raises the question of how other faculty and faculty development coordinators can encourage their colleagues to be open to strengthening their teaching on the basis of new pedagogical research and theory.

## POSSIBLE DISCUSSION QUESTIONS

1. What are Professor Lee's objections to revising syllabi or engaging in collaboration? Are any of them justifiable? Are any of them not justifiable? What are his basic assumptions about academic change in general?

2. How widespread is his attitude?

3. How can faculty and administration deal with people like Professor Lee? Are there ways to convince the Lees of academia at least to try new approaches to teaching?

4. What can administrators and other faculty learn from people like Professor Lee?

5. Is this an issue of Professor Lee's academic freedom?

6. Do you sympathize with Professor Lee? How would you respond to him?

# The Fly in the Ointment

Ted Henson braced himself as he entered the office of Professor Elder Lee—resident malcontent/dissident on the Liberal Arts faculty. He already knew what the reaction would be, but he had his job to do.

"Good morning, Elder," he said, as he stood in the doorway. "I trust you got the chairman's e-mail message about the staff meeting Friday." He knew Lee had and was ready for combat. Lee attended meetings only when he thought there was a chance for some verbal ballistics. "We want to talk about the proposal to collaborate on revising syllabi." Ted had overheard the faculty's reactions to the memo in the staff room, and the chances for pyrotechnics were pretty good.

Professor Elder Fenwick Lee barely acknowledged Ted's presence, but couldn't resist an unmistakable smirk. "Who the hell are you kidding, Henson? We know the syllabus/collaboration business was your idea. You must have been reading more of that English Journal crap. We don't need that high school junk in college. Remember when they tried to make us write syllabi with behavioral objectives? That was fun. Remember the one I tried to insert in my syllabus for English Lit I? 'After reading Lycidas, eighty percent of the students will weep copiously for at least fifteen minutes.' Yeah, I loved those behavioral objectives."

"Look, Elder, I know how you feel, but we voted on this issue at the last meeting. No one objected then. I know it's a pain, but we have an accreditation evaluation coming up next spring. We need to cooperate on this. Whether we like it or not, we are going to have to overhaul our goals and objectives, and syllabi have to reflect them." The chairman had not been equivocal in his message.

Henson waited for the reaction he knew was coming; he was not disappointed. Though Lee was somewhat daunted by the chairman himself, he had no compunction about rebuking the vice-chairman, especially one who had been his humble office-mate for seven years.

"Henson, you're letting your vice-chairmanship go to your head. I knew you when you still recognized administrative b.s. when you saw—or smelled—it. I'll level with you. I'm going to fight this because, first of all, it's phoney. Hell, you just said that we were doing it to impress the accreditation team. Six months after the evaluation, we won't even remember what we so pretentiously penned in—excuse me, *keyboarded* in."

Henson shifted self-consciously in the doorway—he certainly did remember those irreverent but exciting conversations. But he wasn't about to let Lee use their old familiarity to distract him. He made a move to ease himself away and down the hall, but Lee hadn't even noticed his old office-mate's discomfiture. His rhetoric was warming up, having been rehearsed all morning.

"Secondly," he declaimed, "I think it's an unwarranted invasion of my classroom. I don't like other people poking their noses into my classes. Hell, I've been teaching some of these classes for nearly twenty years! I know what I'm doing. Look at my student evaluations. Who does any better? I think I know the real reason for the new syllabi dialogue. And don't tell me that it hasn't occurred to you, Mr. Vice-chairman: the administration wants these damned things as a means of leverage for getting rid of teachers who don't tow the line. And guess who that would be?"

Henson barely suppressed a smile, but his administrative demeanor quickly assumed control. What could he say? He didn't even acknowledge the accusation. Besides, as solidly tenured as Lee was, nothing short of shooting the chairman would ever threaten his job. Again, he made a gesture of escape.

But like the Ancient Mariner, Lee held him with his glittering eye and rumbled on. "But what really gets to me is that we never take a stand and fight these incursions on academic freedom. I won't be docile; we don't all have to march to the same beat. I know I am a good teacher; I don't need to move in lockstep formation with the great flock of academic sheep in this college. My method of teaching demands flexibility. I always know the destination, even though I m not sure of the route each time I begin a new class. This collaborative (that's the new buzz word, isn't it?) syllabus workshop is just another sneaky way to get us all into harness."

Henson was beginning to lose patience. "Look, Elder. I don't make the rules. We need to get ready for the evaluation. We will be held accountable for what we say we're doing in this school. Our syllabi are going to have to wash. That's it."

"I don't aim to be tied to the obligations of a syllabus like one of the 'model' works of art that you sent us. It's a legal contract. If I want to modify or even change my grading system, for instance, I want to keep that license. The way things are going, students are going to sue us if we don't do everything just the way we have it chiseled into our syllabi—if it's to their advantage, of course. I like to leave my grading system less than well defined. There are too many intangibles to have my criteria all delineated. This isn't high school, Henson. Let's treat students like adults and academics.

"And just look at one of the prize models you sent us. Have you really looked at them? It's got aims, general goals, specific goals, enabling goals, and probably even field goals. This is ostentation at its finest. A *tour de force*! And the bibliographies! Did you check the bibliographies? One of them has over a hundred entries. Why? Are they for the students? I doubt it. Are they for the administrators? Maybe. Are they for the accreditation teams? I'll bet on it." Henson looked at his watch.

"And look at some of those ten-page masterpieces. You really believe that the students are going to read them? Come on, Henson, get your head out of the clouds—or wherever you're keeping it. Join the real world. Come back from Cloud Cuckooland and join the people in the trenches. This syllabus collaboration stuff is just another fad. Don't forget those behavioral objectives."

Henson, a man of great reserve and dignity, resisted the impulse for confrontation and said simply, "See you at the meeting, Elder. It's always a pleasure talking to you."

But on his way down the hall, he found himself entertaining certain qualms about his heretofore unswerving defense of tenure.

# Risky Business

*by Lesley K. Cafarelli*
The Collaboration for the Advancement of College Teaching & Learning

## ABSTRACT

This case is about a department chair faced with decisions about a tenure-track professor in a department rife with political tensions about the evaluation of teaching. While the junior faculty member has received positive evaluations in the past and has been involved in faculty development activities, the chair is accosted by concerns from a complaining student and an entrenched senior professor, as well as a mandate on evaluation from the university's new vice-president.

## POSSIBLE DISCUSSION QUESTIONS

1. Should Terry be concerned about Ben's complaint? Should he tell Amanda about the complaint, and if so, how?

2. What role should Ted's views play in the preparation and review of Amanda's tenure dossier?

3. How should Terry respond to the vice-president's mandate concerning the evaluation of teaching?

4. What is your opinion of the system Terry's department uses to decide on merit pay? How might it be improved?

5. How would Terry respond to the vice-president's request for evidence of "how the candidate meets department objectives and standards for good teaching?"

6. What role, if any, might Amanda's work with the Center for Teaching and Learning play in her tenure application? Why?

# Risky Business

Terry Jones leaned back in his chair and took a deep breath. Here it was June 12th, and he had nearly survived his first full year as chair of the history department at Northfield State University. And what a year! He had agreed to the job reluctantly, recruited by a few colleagues and the dean—it was his "turn," they argued. Once persuaded, though, he took the job seriously, managing not only the day-to-day tasks, but shepherding the department's student assessment plan to completion with only a little faculty grumbling and beginning discussions for the department's tenth-year review, scheduled for the next year. It had been really hectic, what with a new academic vice-president and all the administrative talk about "accountability."

Now, with a year under his belt, he felt ready to shift into full gear and hoped to leave his mark by helping to strengthen the department. It had been hard to watch both the teaching and scholarship slipping in recent years as three of the most energetic faculty were lured away to more attractive positions and several others had dug in their heels about curriculum or were marking time till retirement. "Once Amanda Elliott is tenured," he mused, "we'll have more momentum. She's really interested in innovative teaching, and her contacts in the international community could help, too. Maybe we can rejuvenate the old departmental seminars...." He drifted back to his first few years on the faculty, when occasional gatherings of faculty and students with outside speakers sparked lively debates about the most recent scholarship (at least other people's scholarship, he mused). "Well, first things first; Amanda will be in tomorrow to get advice on preparing her tenure file for next year. I'd better take a look at those course evaluations...."

A knock startled Terry from his reverie, and Ben Adams stuck his head around the door. Ben was a junior majoring in the department, a steady but (Terry had found) rather uninspired student. Invited in, he slumped across the room, engineer boots thumping on the linoleum floor and backpack dangling, and fell into a chair. "Boy, am I pooped!" he said. "I just turned in my last final, and I've had to work thirty hours this week."

"That's tough," Terry responded. "I'm sure you did your best."

"Yeah, well, I sure tried," said Ben. "But that's the thing, Professor Jones. I really knocked myself out for Professor Elliott's Civil War seminar. Boy, we had a ton of reading! But I just picked up our final group project and my final grade—she sure does turn 'em around fast, at least—it's a C, and I don't get it. I mean, I did good, solid work and kept up and all. So did most of the others, but, well, we had one sloucher. She does this collaborative learning thing, you know—I mean Professor Elliott—and, well, why should I have to pay with my grade for somebody else's laziness? Why can't she just do lectures and exams like the other profs? Do we have to be guinea pigs while she figures out how to teach?"

Terry thought back to the visit that Ted Johnson, a senior member of the department, had made to one of Amanda's classes earlier in the year. "She had the students sitting in groups, and they were trying to figure out what they were supposed to do," he had written. "It was so noisy, no one could think. She spent the period just walking around and mingling with the students, and there was little evidence of mastery of her subject." He wasn't surprised to hear this from Ted, whose own reputation was based on his extraordinary lectures, which had even won him the Alumni Award for Outstanding Teaching. Ted (James Theodore Johnson, who published and lectured widely on 18th-century British naval history), was a celebrity on campus, and students flocked to his introductory courses. Terry turned to Ben.

"Actually, a lot of faculty use collaborative learning now, just not so much in our department. I do myself sometimes. Working with a group of people can be hard, though. Have you talked to Professor Elliott about your work? If you have questions, maybe she can help you," Terry answered, hoping to avoid second-guessing Amanda's judgment.

"Yeah, well, not really. I mean, I did ask some questions about her grading policies at the beginning, but, well, there didn't seem to be much point. She kept saying how it was important for us to work in teams, that that's how it is in the real world, you know. And she wanted us to help set the grading standards, grade our group's work and all that. Isn't that what she's being paid to do?" Ben seemed to be growing more irritable.

"Well, Ben, I understand that it's hard when different faculty have different approaches to teaching. But that's OK as long as students are learning the material, and collaborative learning can be a good way to help students learn. If something isn't clear, though, it's up to you to check it out. I can talk with Professor Elliott about the course overall, but you should follow up with her if you have questions about your work."

"Well, there's not much point. I mean, she's not going to change my grade and all; she's got her mind made up. I just won't take any more courses from her. I just wanted you to know what's going on. I think it stinks, and I'm not the only one." Ben rose and walked out the door.

"Disgruntled student," Terry thought. But a half-hour later, when Terry finished reading Amanda's student evaluations, he thought maybe there was a problem. Ben was not, in fact, "the only one." A look at the past year's course enrollments confirmed Terry's uncertain memory Amanda's enrollments had dropped, including several student withdrawals.

Walking home that night from campus, Terry thought about the meeting he would have with Amanda the next morning. He liked Amanda and thought she had a lot to offer the department and the university. Her third-year review had gone very smoothly. At that time, she had already published a few articles in reputable journals and was well underway revising her dissertation into a book on the role of black women in the Confederate south; the book was now out and had been received well by most of the scholarly community, although one prominent scholar had questioned her sources. She and two undergraduate research assistants had presented several times at meetings of the Organization of American Historians and other disciplinary groups. She had also served on several university committees, including the new Council on Liberal Education appointed by the vice-president, and actively advocated for women faculty, staff, and students as a board member for the campus Women's Center.

As a new faculty member, Amanda had participated voluntarily, with the support of Bob Dawkins, the previous department chair, in a new mentoring program run by the university's Center for Teaching and Learning. Through the program, she had been matched with John Harris, a professor in the English department, who had been at Northfield State for almost thirty years and was well respected as a teacher, scholar, and all-round campus "citizen." John had himself experimented successfully with a wide range of teaching methods designed to promote active learning (he joked that it was his second childhood), and the two of them had attended several faculty development workshops and visited each other's classes. They had also worked on teaching portfolios together, using their writing to reflect on and try to solve problems in their teaching. Amanda spoke enthusiastically about the coaching John and the other senior faculty mentors had provided, and through the biweekly meetings, she had gotten to know a lot of the other newer faculty. The program provided a safe space to talk openly about problems the faculty were having in teaching and other adjustments to the campus and community, she said. She had even exchanged day care with other faculty in the group.

Terry recalled how lonely he had felt during his first years on campus and envied Amanda for the support the group provided. His senior colleagues in history had not been very welcoming; he'd relied mainly on Shirley, the department secretary, to find his way around. Fresh from graduate school and eager to discuss his research, he learned quickly that the faculty spoke seldom about their scholarship and even less about their teaching. What seemed at first to be detachment soon felt like competitiveness; soon, he came to recognize outright factions, especially over decisions regarding curriculum and hiring. Funny, not much had changed in his eighteen years.

Of the twelve full-time faculty in the department (nine men and three women), one was visiting, three were tenure-track, and eight were tenured, including five who had been there for over twenty-three years. In recent years, three faculty had left (including a woman and an African-American man), and two others had not received tenure, one, lacking department support (disagreement over scholarly bias) and the other with department support, but overturned by the previous academic vice-president. Most of the rest were good, solid teachers who took care in preparing their lectures and recitations. Terry and one or two others had also attended a few of the faculty development workshops offered by the Center for Teaching and Learning— or the "Center for Torture and Learning," as Ted Johnson had quipped.

Year after year, as long as Terry could remember, Ted ranked at the top of the annual department review, which was used to assign merit pay. A strange system, Terry thought, and he longed to change it. Each year, every member of the department rated every other member on three criteria, weighted equally—number of pages published in refereed journals in the discipline (interdisciplinary and other journals did not count), mean scores on the standardized final student evaluation submitted for one course per semester, and committee service. And each year, the same faculty ended up in roughly the same rank order—Ted first, then Bob Dawkins (the former chair), Phil, Terry himself, Amanda…. There had been some talk about evaluating teaching in other ways— some faculty questioned how students could judge their teaching—but the discussions had gone nowhere.

Terry knew that Amanda was interested in using parts of her teaching portfolio in her tenure file. He wondered how that would fly.

The next morning, Terry arrived at his office to find a letter from the new academic vice-president to all deans and department chairs.

> Recently, the legislature has asked all institutions in the state to provide clear evidence of improvements in undergraduate teaching, faculty productivity, and student satisfaction as a basis for determining our budget in the next biennium. Since Northfield State University distinguishes itself as a teaching institution providing graduates who will contribute to our economy and quality of life, we have both an opportunity and a responsibility to lead the way in documenting the quality of our teaching.
>
> As you know, good teaching already counts for close to half of the points awarded in promotion and tenure decisions. Effective immediately,

however, departments will be expected to demonstrate the following when recommending candidates for tenure to my office:

1) Evidence of the candidate's superior teaching effectiveness based on student evaluations.

2) Evidence that the candidate is contributing positively to the number of departmental majors.

3) Evidence for how the candidate meets departmental objectives and standards for good teaching.

In addition, as a strong proponent of teaching improvement, I have asked the University's Center for Teaching and Learning to provide an annual roster of faculty who have participated in its teaching consultation and other programs, along with evidence of improvements made. All relevant information will be included in making the final decision on future promotion and tenure candidates.

Suddenly, Terry noticed Amanda waiting quietly in the doorway.

"A look only a mother could love," she observed, alluding to his face, which was knotted in anguish. "Ready to talk tenure?"

# To 'B' or Not To 'B':
# A Case of Academic Appeal

*by Benedict J. Arogyaswamy*
University of South Dakota

## ABSTRACT

This case involves a student who feels that the professor wasted class time, leading to a poor grade for the student. Several issues crop up—cultural biases, academic freedom, and the fairness of academic appeal procedures. Sample focus questions are included.

## POSSIBLE DISCUSSION QUESTIONS

1. Should Ashish have agreed to serve on the (specially constituted) grievance committee with his preconceived notions of grade redressal and knowing it was his close friend's grade that was being grieved?

2. Should Ashish, a management professor, have advised Bob in the first place about academic processes in the health care administration department?

3. Do you think Sandy has a legitimate case, and is she correct in pursuing an academic appeal procedure?

4. Would a grade grievance filed against you make you defensive? How would you reduce defensive behavior in a case such as this?

# To 'B' or Not To 'B': A Case of Academic Appeal

Ashish Kumar had been teaching management at Midwest College (a small comprehensive liberal arts college) for two years when the dean asked him to serve on a grade grievance committee. Ashish had heard that students could grieve a grade and ask for a higher grade. This, of course, was unheard of in his home country of India. In India you could not grieve a grade—period.

Still, Ashish agreed to serve on the committee because the dean had asked him to and because he needed a "service" component on his vita. The faculty handbook states that to receive promotion and tenure a faculty member has to be rated "excellent" on two of three components (i.e., teaching, research, and service) that faculty are rated on and at least "satisfactory" on the third. Though Ashish was a couple of years away from the tenure decision and knew that research and teaching were more important in terms of a favorable decision, he felt that this might be a good time to start building his service record.

"Should a student grieve a grade? I wouldn't if I were a student," thought Ashish, who had received several B's during his graduate work. He had always considered professors to be unbiased and objective, and believed that the grade received was a fair reflection of the work put in by the student.

Ashish met the dean the next day and asked, "Who is the professor in this case?" The dean said, "Well, it is Bob Malone. Hey, Ash—I have to run now—I have to meet with the provost. Stop by some other time if you have any more questions. I'll send you a memo with the names of the other committee members and the date for your first meeting. OK?" The dean hurried away as Ashish nodded dumbly.

Bob Malone, who had joined Midwest a year ago, was a good friend of Ashish's. Ashish had been on the search committee and later when Bob moved into town, they started playing racquetball together and had found that their families got along really well too. In fact, Ashish had shown Bob the ropes and had even advised him on grading policies and on dealing with administration and students! He remembered telling Bob, "Don't worry, the administration is really good about student grievances—they never support the student! You know, a couple of years ago when Denny (the Assistant Dean) had a grade grievance, the faculty committee went by the letter of the law and insisted that they would check only that there wasn't any discriminatory grading. They didn't even look at his grading policy—which left a lot to be desired—and I'm being kind!" Now Bob was in trouble. "Did I goof up? Did I tell him stuff that led him into this mess?" wondered Ashish.

Later that week, Ashish received a memo from the dean detailing the complete grievance procedure and specifying the exact nature of the complaint. Ashish found out that the student, Sandy Brown, had received a C in her Healthcare Systems class, and had noted several reasons why she thought that she deserved at least a B. She was pursuing the academic appeal procedure published in the Student Handbook.

To summarize, Sandy felt that Professor Malone had wasted time in class. She felt that material that was not mentioned on the syllabus was required on the final exam, and students had not been given adequate warning of the content of the exam.

Sandy's letter to the dean outlined all the problems she had with Bob Malone's class and included a description of her efforts to get her grievances addressed by Professor Malone and by the chair of the department of healthcare administration.

When Ashish spoke to Bob, Bob was mostly concerned about how the appeal would affect his academic career. Bob felt that the appeal might send a message to the administration that he did not do a good job in the classroom. Ashish tried to console Bob saying, "It doesn't make such a big difference—for promotion and tenure they mainly go by teaching evaluations. I'm sure this will be treated as just a blip on a good record."

# To Tell or Not To Tell

*by Shamsul Huda, Argiro L. Morgan, and William Serban*
Xavier University of Louisiana

## ABSTRACT

While working on a collaborative project with a male colleague, a young female faculty member inadvertently learns from a student that her colleague harbors prejudice against a minority group. Confronting her colleague would violate the confidentiality of the student's disclosure as well as endanger the collaborative endeavor. Seniority, diversity, gender, and tenure criteria are some issues addressed in this case.

## POSSIBLE DISCUSSION QUESTIONS

1. Why does Julie feel she cannot speak up about Professor Sampson? Should she speak up?

2. How should Julie have responded to the student who gave her the information about Burt?

3. How can Michelle help Julie?

4. Does the cultural context of the campus have any impact on how you perceive the issues involved in this case?

## To Tell or Not To Tell

"May I interrupt you for a moment, Michelle? I have something I must discuss with someone, and I guess you're it," Julie Anton said, as she walked into Michelle Dickerson's office and quietly closed the door.

Michelle was hidden behind a stack of books and papers. Recognizing Julie's voice, she shifted her attention from a pile of student essays she had just begun to grade and looked up in surprise. Usually, faculty who were working with Michelle's Partners-in-Learning Project discussed what they observed about teaching and student learning over coffee and dessert once a month in each other's homes. It was unusual for them to come to her office with a problem, and a problem it must be, judging by the edge in Julie's voice and the furrow on her brow. Michelle wondered what it could be. Of all the faculty pairs in the Project, she least expected difficulties with Julie and Burt. Julie was a young, eager instructor in political science and her partner, Burt Sampson, a more experienced fifth-year history professor who was well regarded by students and other faculty. Michelle stood up to greet Julie with a warm smile on her face.

"Of course you may interrupt me, Julie. In fact, I've been reading these essays for quite awhile. You've given me a good reason to let up for a bit. But you seem bothered by something. Can I help?"

"Michelle, I've run across a difficulty I really don't know how to handle, or even if it should be handled at all," Julie stammered.

Michelle waited patiently for Julie to continue, but instead, Julie simply sat, looking down at her hands, seemingly trying to find either the words or courage to go on. After a ten-second wait, which seemed interminable to Michelle, she hesitantly asked, "Is there a problem between you and Burt working together, Julie?"

"Oh, no. Our weekly meetings are cordial, and I admit, I'm learning more about teaching from him than he learned from me when he sat in on my course last term. You know, Michelle, he's a wonderful teacher."

"Yes, I've often heard that from students and from some other faculty."

"Well, he's not just organized, you know. He's like an actor on stage. The lectures are perfectly timed to be completed in one class period, and he uses stories, anecdotes, slides and even tapes at times to keep students really interested in history. Teaching's not his problem."

Again, Michelle waited. This time she decided to give Julie the time to reveal the reason for her obvious distress. "Well, you know that I speak to Burt's students regularly during the semester," Julie finally offered.

"Right, Julie, that's a key part of the project. Did a student comment on something that bothered you about Burt's teaching?"

Hesitantly Julie replied, "Yes, someone did."

Michelle felt somewhat relieved. "Well, you know, that does happen in this project. You're bound to hear some negative comments about even the best of teachers. In fact, sometimes faculty teams can learn the most from students who don't mind speaking up about their hidden dissatisfactions."

"Well, it's not that simple, this time. Of course, we've both heard some student comments that we used to alter our teaching somewhat during the year, though, I admit, I was the one who had the most to learn from student reactions. But, this time, well, a student hit on a rather sensitive issue."

Inwardly, Michelle braced herself. She had a vague notion that perhaps the issue of sexual harassment or sexual preference had surfaced. And on a Southern, Christian campus, that could cause quite a scene, or even wreck the faculty development project she was heading. But she said nothing. Instead, she leaned toward Julie, hoping to encourage her to go on with her story by being quietly receptive.

Julie continued, "You know, I'm quite aware that our conversations with students are to be confidential. We're not to reveal anything that could identify a student, and also administrators aren't to be involved—except in broad terms—with what we're learning."

"Yes, that's one of the strengths of the project," Michelle answered. "In that way, students can be honest, and faculty aren't afraid that any weaknesses they have could be used to hurt them in tenure and promotion decisions. But evidently, Julie, what the student said has caused quite a quandary for you, hasn't it?"

"Well, yes, and I guess I can trust you enough to tell you what happened, because I really need advice," stammered Julie. "You see," she went on, "I was speaking to a student about Burt's availability in his office, and suddenly the student said, 'Dr. Sampson is a great guy to chat with in his office. Boy, when he gets talking nasty about Muslims, he loses all track of time.'

"You know, Michelle, this really caught me off guard. In the American history class I'm visiting, Burt is using a chronological approach, and he's talking now about the Jacksonian era. So far, Arabs and Muslims haven't been touched on at all. I tried to hide my surprise and said that I didn't know that Dr. Sampson had any particular interest in the Islamic religion. The student suddenly seemed embarrassed, like he had let the cat out of the bag."

Now Michelle was confused. "You mean that the talk between the student and Burt touched on sensitive issues?"

"That's exactly what I mean," replied Julie. "At first, I didn't realize what the student was getting at. He was caught off guard by my comment about Burt, and if I hadn't been meeting with this student for a couple of months, I think he would have just managed to 'hem and haw' a bit. But I feigned interest to encourage him to go on.

"And then the student actually said, 'Well, you've got to know that a lot of us feel that we're letting too damn many immigrants into this country. And at this university—which is supposed to be Christian—there are just too many Arab teachers. Somebody has to speak up, Dr. Anton.'

"I asked, 'And you think that Dr. Sampson does?'

"'Well, only in private,' he said. 'And I gotta say, I don't know if it's an immigrant thing with him 'cause he doesn't hit on Orientals. But you must know how the prof feels about the Muslims. And you gotta agree with him too. After all, you're a woman.'

"'A woman?' I responded.

"'Sure,' he said. 'I mean, Dr. Sampson gets just livid when he talks about how Muslims make women wear veils, and how they can have a lot of wives. Why, they're treated just like concubines, he says.'

"Then, I asked the student if he really knew any of the Muslim faculty or their families here at the university, and he said, 'No way. And I don't want to either.'

"'Why?' I asked. And then the student started talking about guess what, Michelle? Terrorism! He went into a tirade about the Persian Gulf War, the Arab Oil Embargo, and the cutting off of hands under Islamic law. I've never seen this student get so animated.

"He then went on to say that you couldn't really trust Muslims because beneath that controlled exterior is a 'fanatical terrorist.' Those were his exact words, Michelle, a 'fanatical terrorist!'" Julie paused.

"How did you reply, Julie?" Michelle asked with concern.

"Well, if I wasn't in this Partners-in-Learning Project, I would have said a lot. The student's ideas were way off base, to say the least. But here his views seemed to be reinforced by my own 'partner' in the project. I'm supposed to just listen to students and then bring comments back to Burt. So the only thing I asked was if Dr. Sampson shared all of the student's views. And you know what the student said? He said, 'Sure. But Dr. Sampson knows when to keep his mouth shut and when not to, because with all that diversity movement on campus, he doesn't want to get in trouble.'"

Julie stammered, "Well, now you have it. I feel trapped. What can I do? I know I'm supposed to speak to Burt about our student interviews. But if I confront him, he could just deny it, and maybe identify the student as well. Would he take it out on the student? And it certainly could ruin the relationship I thought we were building. Besides that, Michelle, Burt has a solid reputation among a number of faculty at this university, and this is only my first year teaching here. If I let this issue go, who knows what else could surface? Do you think this is just the tip of the iceberg? But as an historian and supposedly an educated person, if those really are his views—wow! Now I feel I don't know him at all. Did he just get in this project because he's up for tenure next year? And what about his effects on our students? My goodness, Michelle, what am I supposed to do...?"

Julie's voice trailed off, as she looked at Michelle for guidance.

# Unpopular Senior Professor

*by Bruce L. Smith*
University of South Dakota

## ABSTRACT

A department chair struggles to manage a department high in faculty turnover that also has a senior professor who is unpopular with students and very resistant to change. The professor says his high standards are resisted by students who prefer easier instructors. The students say the professor is rigid and more interested in preserving his image of being tough than with helping them to learn.

## POSSIBLE DISCUSSION QUESTIONS

1. How might a tenured full professor be motivated to be more open to change with regard to his or her teaching methods and other changes within a department?

2. What are the obstacles to change within your department?

3. Are you acquainted with "change agents," people who are successful at helping organizations to change? What skills and techniques do they use as facilitators?

4. Do people always resist change? How can resistance to change be minimized?

# Unpopular Senior Professor

"Again, I must deal with Bill's low enrollments," John McClure mused. He was annoyed with himself for being both surprised and frustrated by the recurring situation.

John McClure was the chair of the Department of Journalism and Public Communication at the College of the Prairie. He had held the position for two years.

The department had a faculty of seven, including five untenured assistant professors, one tenured associate professor (John himself), and one tenured full professor. Faculty ranged in age from twenty-nine to sixty-three.

Faculty turnover in the department had been a huge problem for six or seven years. New faculty usually stayed only a year or two. Many were ABDs, and left when they completed their dissertations and were awarded their doctoral degrees.

The revolving-door turnover of faculty had been a frustration for students, other faculty, and the university administration. Students complained that faculty left so quickly it was hard to take more than a class or two from instructors before they were gone. John thought this was an exaggeration, but he sympathized with students who found it difficult to build and sustain relationships with faculty.

Several issues contributed to the problem. The university was not a prestigious institution. Ambitious faculty used it as a stopping-off point on the way to larger research institutions. Low salaries and minimal support for research and faculty development were also factors. Internal departmental politics also contributed to the turnover. A couple of faculty members had told John they hoped to leave because they were weary of the in-fighting and uncollegial atmosphere in the department.

The only constant on the faculty was Bill Main. Bill was an institution in the department and on campus. He had been on the faculty for many years. While he too had applied for positions elsewhere, he had not found one and believed himself to be the victim of age discrimination.

Bill was the senior member of the faculty. He was a tenured full professor, sixty-three years old. Bill had chaired the department for several years before being asked by the Dean to step down from the position. He remembered his tenure as chair as being the department's "golden age." He had made clear his intention to continue working until his health failed. Divorced and childless, he said that his work kept him young and healthy.

Bill was John McClure's current concern. Bill's student evaluations were consistently low. While students seemed to think that he was familiar with course content, they gave him very low marks in most other areas. Written evaluation comments included remarks such as "Dr. Main is so concerned about being a hard-ass, he doesn't care whether we are learning or not." Bill relished his image as a "hard-ass."

"I'm the toughest instructor in this department," he told John. "That's why students don't take classes from me."

Bill's elective classes were canceled regularly because enrollments were too low to justify offering them. The university said classes with fewer than ten students should not be offered, but Bill's elective classes seldom reached enrollments of ten. Now, John McClure had to decide how to deal with another of Bill's underenrolled classes for the coming semester.

John had dealt with the problem last semester by having Bill teach required classes only. He had already scheduled Bill to teach two senior level required courses for the coming semester. He also decided to schedule an extra section of the Introduction to Mass Communication class for Bill to teach, because it was also required.

That solution satisfied the administrative problem of low enrollments, but it left other problems. Bill complained about having to teach the same required classes over and over again. It also meant that important electives were not being taught because they had to be canceled. Examples included International Communications, Media Criticism, and Media Sales, three electives that Bill had been scheduled to teach in recent semesters, but which had been canceled because of low enrollments.

John confided to his dean, Jerry Balsam, that he felt he was between a rock and a hard place.

"The only way I can give Bill a full load is to have him teach the same required classes all the time," he said. "The students grumble about having to take classes from Bill, but they have no choice. Some of those required classes don't really need to be offered every semester. They could be taught less often with larger class sizes, but then what would I do with Bill?"

The dean offered no advice except to say it had been a continuing problem, and the important thing was to keep everyone teaching full loads with at least ten students in every class.

Everyone was unhappy with the present situation. John felt the present use of faculty resources was inefficient. Bill hated teaching the same classes every semester. And the students were unhappy because they were forced to take classes from Bill.

John wondered if there were a way to help Bill teach more effectively. The problems seemed to arise from both Bill's didactic presentation style and his aggressive demeanor.

A graduate student confided to John that some of Bill's behavior in class scared her. "His classes don't feel safe to me," she said. "I don't feel I can disagree with him or question him. I feel safe only if I just sit and listen."

"Enrollments in my classes are low because I maintain rigorous standards, and students know they have to meet those standards," Bill told his colleagues at a faculty meeting.

David Burke, a two-year veteran of the department and one of the faculty members who hoped to find another job, barely contained his anger. "Are you implying the standards of other faculty in this department are not rigorous?" he asked.

"I'm only saying some less-experienced faculty would rather be buddies with the students than be demanding of them," Bill replied. He rather enjoyed such confrontations, seeing them as an opportunity to match wits with the junior members of the faculty.

"You can see in the grading reports I consistently give the lowest grades in this department," Bill boasted. "Students know they can't get an easy A from me, and it scares them away."

"I think your accusations are exceedingly unfair," David responded. "You have no idea what the rest of us are doing in our classes, especially since we have to carry the burden of teaching most of the students in this department."

At that point, John intervened to stop the conflict from escalating further. He felt his neck muscles tighten from the tension and wondered if he had any aspirin left in his briefcase.

Criticism of Bill Main's teaching was not limited to students and his colleagues on the faculty. John had heard criticism from off-campus professionals, who claimed Bill taught outdated material. When John had sat in on Bill's classes, however, the content seemed contemporary, although Bill's presentation style was dreary.

Bill was also an obstacle to any efforts to change curriculum and policies. He opposed change generally, and particularly opposed changing policies and curriculum requirements put in place when he was chair. His most common argument was that the changes would make the academic program less rigorous and damage its integrity. He implied that those who argued for change were promoting a lowering of standards and said he intended to remain a vocal champion for high standards. "Am I the only faculty member in this department who cares about standards?" Bill asked at a curriculum committee meeting.

Sally Smith, a first-year faculty member, politely asked everyone not to personalize the discussion.

"I believe it is unfair to characterize the proposed changes as an assault on standards," she said. "They are intended to fix policies that don't work or to implement curriculum changes that will make the program more reflective of contemporary thinking in the field. Times change, the profession is changing, and our curriculum and policies must also change from time to time."

Privately, several members of the faculty expressed their frustrations. "He hides behind the standards argument to deflect change of every kind," David complained bitterly. "I'm tired of having my standards impugned. He finds a reason to fight every change, no matter how small and insignificant."

John McClure was an experienced manager. He spent four years chairing another department of comparable size. He had also spent almost fifteen years as a newspaper editor and publisher. Mid-life, he decided to return to school to earn his Ph.D. so he could teach.

"I don't think we would have this problem in industry," John told his wife. "If someone didn't keep current, couldn't change or couldn't carry his weight, he would be out the door. But the university is a unique culture. Faculty have the protection of tenure. The general institutional resistance to change makes it easier for people like Bill to hang on. He's not the only faculty member on the campus who feels like a hero for resisting change."

John wondered how an academic unit could recreate its culture to be more accepting of change.

"How can we help Bill and other faculty members learn new teaching methods? How can we make curriculum, policy, and other kinds of changes feel safe to faculty so there is less resistance to them?"

John was convinced that if he could find the answer to the puzzle of change, the department might be a more positive place, with less turnover. Even the problem of Bill's underenrolled classes might be solved.

# Wendy Lamb

*by Tom Mason and Melissa Shepard*
University of St. Thomas

## ABSTRACT

A capable junior faculty member participates in a faculty development program designed to focus on one of her physics courses. To her dismay, students show little enthusiasm for the course, and several drop. As a result, the professor is too upset to take advantage of the mentoring opportunity offered by her faculty development partner.

## POSSIBLE DISCUSSION QUESTIONS

1. Should Bob have seen the problems coming? Or were they unpredictable? Are they "problems" or simply part of the experience of becoming a teacher?

2. How should Wendy respond to recent events in her physics class? Are there lessons she should learn for future classes?

3. How might Bob be helpful to Wendy? Should he push her to let him go ahead with his meeting with her students? Should he back off and give her some time to work through the problems on her own? How does a faculty development coordinator respond to a faculty colleague in such a situation?

# Wendy Lamb

As Bob Jeffries sat down wearily in his office, he was struck by how much things had changed since he and Wendy Lamb had first talked. Bob had just returned from Wendy's office where he had stopped in to confirm his visit to her physics class. Wendy had seemed very distressed about recent events in the class and was unwilling to proceed with his class visit. In fact, it was not clear to Bob whether she was postponing the visit or canceling it. Now he sat gazing out the window and recalling the sequence of events that had taken such an unexpected turn.

The summer before, during a faculty development workshop, Bob had mentioned that the Instructional Support Center, of which he was the coordinator, would begin offering a "classroom consulting" service to help faculty assess their teaching. Bob, the coordinator of the Center, was also to be one of the consultants who would team with an instructor and focus on a single course. Wendy had immediately asked him to work through the process with her in her introductory physics class. Thanks to her, Bob had just signed his first client and was about to become a classroom consultant.

Wendy was starting her fourth year in the Physics Department and hoping to be tenured in a couple of years. Bob was pleased and perhaps a little surprised, when they talked in late August, at how willingly Wendy shared her course syllabus, assignments, and even student evaluations from earlier semesters. As he read over the materials, Bob could see that she had no reason to be insecure. Her course materials were organized, thorough, and interesting, and her students clearly recognized her energy and commitment and considered her a very capable and caring, yet demanding, teacher. Early in the fall term they met again to discuss Bob's reactions to the course materials and student comments.

"Wendy, these are great student evaluations. They're very positive. You must have some others tucked away that you'd rather forget about." Bob chuckled when he said this so it would not sound like an accusation.

"No I don't! Why do you say that?" Wendy seemed a little insulted by the comment.

"It's just that I assume anyone who has taught a tough subject like physics for three years has encountered at least one class of malcontents," Bob hurried to explain. He did not want his attempt at humor to make Wendy defensive.

"Well, I always have one or two a semester, but never a whole class." Wendy's smile returned and Bob continued, silently chiding himself to try to avoid any further blunders.

"After reading your syllabus and assignments, I can see that you might win over even the most skeptical student. I've seen syllabi that read like legal contracts, but yours is more like an invitation to share your enthusiasm for physics." Wendy looked a little embarrassed by the praise. "So, the next step is for me to recommend you tell your students in advance that I'm coming and why."

"That's fine, Bob. How about next Wednesday? I'm looking forward to this. I've never had another teacher visit my class before." The statement seemed not to carry even a trace of anxiety or defensiveness, and Bob was delighted by her enthusiasm and openness to the process.

Bob visited Wendy's class the following week. He was aware that she made eye contact with him only a couple of times, and he suspected she was a little nervous because he was there. Nevertheless, it became even clearer, as he sat in her class, that Wendy was a skilled teacher who enjoyed both the subject matter and the contact with the students. Later, as he prepared to meet with her to discuss his observations, he was glad to have the opportunity to reinforce such effective teaching.

"Hi, Wendy. Come in and have a seat. I enjoyed your class." Wendy smiled as she sat down. She seemed very relaxed. "It's been a long time since I was in a physics class, but you explained the material so clearly and thoroughly that I found it all coming back very quickly. I had to remind myself that I was there to focus on you and the students, not to review my knowledge of physics."

"That's nice to hear. I was a little nervous at first—which surprised me—but then I relaxed and was okay. I don't think the students were affected by your being there. Do you?"

Wendy seemed so confident and at ease discussing the class Bob had visited that he found himself wondering if, in his fourth year of teaching, he would have been so comfortable with a senior faculty member critiquing his class. He continued, "No. I sensed they were a little curious, but not really distracted. I noticed they were clustered in the front of the room with only one or two in the back. Is that typical?"

"Yes. The first day of class I told them I wanted them to sit close to the front, that they would be more involved in the class that way. I haven't had to remind them even once. In fact, the first two rows usually fill up first." Wendy looked a little quizzical, as if she might be surprised that Bob thought this worth noting.

"That's great. They're willing to sit in the front, and they're very attentive. I didn't see any side conversations or anyone gazing out the window." Bob paused briefly before bringing up the one concern he had about the class. Seeing that Wendy looked completely at ease, he just said it directly. "I was puzzled that many of them seemed unable or unwilling to participate in discussion or ask questions." Wendy seemed to tense slightly and her eyes narrowed a little. Bob hoped he had not been too abrupt and blunt.

"I know. I don't know what to make of that. They come to class, they sit in the front, they pay attention and take notes, but only four of them seem actively involved. My major frustration is that I want more students to be more involved."

This was the first time Bob had heard the word "frustration" from Wendy. He also heard a note of frustration creep into her voice. They discussed several ways Wendy might draw the students out and get them to be more active. It was clear this was an issue of some concern and Wendy seemed glad for the suggestions. Bob reminded her of her success with earlier classes and told her he was confident she would make active learners of these students. Glancing briefly at his notes, he realized there was one other issue he wanted to raise.

"There was one thing I noticed: when you asked for a response from the class, your wait time was generally quite short. That's typical, and the students learn they can win the waiting game if they don't want to talk, especially with difficult technical material."

"Oh! I'm surprised. It always seems like such a long wait." Wendy seemed to ponder this for a moment. "I guess I'll have to count to ten or something. It's so hard to wait through their silence."

Bob hurried to reassure her. "Yes it is. But try to hold out. Remember the silence makes them just as uncomfortable as it makes you. If you convince them that you'll wait them out, they will begin to respond." Wendy nodded in agreement as she jotted some notes on the paper in front of her. Bob thought this might be a good opportunity to discuss active learning. "One last observation, and it's something I struggle with in my own teaching. You're doing the work at the board and inviting them to ask questions or supply part of a solution to a problem. Do you think you can get them to take a more active role?"

Wendy reminded Bob that she had participated in the Instructional Support Center's cooperative learning workshop and that she had groups working on term projects, but not during class time. She felt constrained by the need to cover material required as preparation for Physics II. Wendy and Bob discussed this apparent conflict a while and Bob offered some suggestions on how to get the students more involved during class time without falling behind the syllabus. The rest of the conversation was easy and pleasant. They confirmed the date for Bob's meeting with her students, and Wendy thanked him for his help and left. Bob sat for a few minutes reflecting on the discussion. He thought it had been very positive, that they had talked through her one real concern about the class, the students' passivity, and that Wendy seemed genuinely pleased when she left.

Two days before he was to meet with her students, Bob decided to drop by Wendy's office. As he walked through the physics department, he smiled to himself and thought how fortunate he was to be working with such a committed, enthusiastic instructor in his first attempt at classroom consulting. He knew his first experience should be with a successful teacher, and he should leave the problem cases for later. Wendy was a successful teacher, no doubt about that! In fact, Bob's only concern was whether this process was useful to both of them or only to him.

Wendy's office door was open and Bob could see her at her desk grading papers. "Hi, Wendy. Got a minute?" She turned and motioned him to the chair beside her desk. He wondered if he had walked in on her rushing to finish her grading before her next class. She looked tense and her smile seemed forced.

Bob decided to quickly confirm his meeting with Wendy's students and then leave so she could get on with her grading. He continued matter-of-factly, "I just stopped by to make sure we're all set for me to meet with your class next Monday. You look busy, so I'll only stay for a moment."

"That's okay. I was going to call you this afternoon, anyway." She paused and seemed to be weighing how she wanted to continue. "I don't know, Bob.... Things aren't going well, and I'm not sure what to do.... Maybe we should wait."

It sounded to Bob like despair in Wendy's voice. He noticed that she looked tired. "What's the problem?"

"I've never had a class like this before. In the past two weeks, eight students have dropped the class. Eight! Six of them before the first exam! I know you and I talked about them not responding to my questions, and I guess I haven't done too well at waiting them out. But I thought things were going well enough in the class. I certainly didn't think eight students would disappear. I thought..."

Bob waited to see if Wendy would finish her statement, but he saw from the look in her eyes that it would remain just a thought. "Wendy," he interrupted, tentatively, "when was the first exam?" He knew that must sound like an odd question, but he was stalling for time trying to figure out how to respond to Wendy's distress, which had caught him completely by surprise.

"Last Wednesday," Wendy said absentmindedly.

"Did any of the students come to see you before they dropped your course?" Bob felt badly for Wendy as he imagined his own reaction if one-third of the students in his class dropped. He hoped getting her to talk through what had happened might help.

"No!" Wendy paused and then continued sounding slightly less agitated. "Well, two of them did. I've always thought of myself as a very approachable teacher. But now I'm wondering if the others are afraid of me."

"That's hard to imagine after reading your student evaluations and visiting your class."

Wendy seemed not to hear Bob's comment as she continued, "I don't think it would bother me so much if the ones who stayed in the class were engaging the material, participating, asking questions. But they aren't. Several of the students admitted to me quite openly that they often come to class without having attempted the assigned problems!"

"At least they're honest with you." Wendy did not respond to Bob's attempt to lighten the mood. She looked glum.

"In every class session, I take questions on the assignment from the previous class. The same three or four students ask questions. The others sit with pencils poised ready to write down what I say. On Monday, after getting just one question on a very difficult assignment, I asked how many had done the homework. Two hands went up! Two!" Wendy's frustration with the students seemed to border on anger. "How do they expect to learn if they refuse to work?"

"What about—" Bob tried to interrupt, to somehow get the conversation moving in a more positive direction, but Wendy continued.

"And there were nine Ds and three Fs on the first exam. That's twelve out of twenty-two. Only three students have come to my office to talk to me. Three! I always write a personal note on the exams of students getting a D or lower urging them to come in and discuss it with me. I also announce this in class when I return the exams. But only three have come to see me!" The more she talked, the more distressed Wendy looked.

"This is definitely different from your experiences in other semesters. What do you think is going on?" The question seemed to bring Wendy back to the present. Her eyes focused again as she looked at him.

"I don't know, Bob. But I'm hurt and upset. I don't feel very confident about my teaching right now."

"I don't blame you for being upset. Can you think of anything that might explain what's going on in class?"

"Well, a group of the better students did come to see me." Wendy's mood seemed to lighten just a little. Bob hoped it meant she was shifting from focusing on her distress to analyzing the situation. "They said they'd had exams in several courses within a very short time. They were having trouble keeping up with the reading and problems I assigned, and working on the course project too."

"Sounds like they're confronting the reality of college life." Although Wendy still looked dejected, her anger seemed to be dissipating. Bob hoped she had talked through it and that they might find something positive in her experience before he mentioned his upcoming meeting with her students. "You know, you sound really down, but I'm sure there are bright spots somewhere in this picture."

Wendy seemed to ponder the idea for a minute. "I guess class went well yesterday. The students were participating." She paused as if revisiting the previous day's class. She relaxed a little, and a trace of a smile reappeared. "There was more interaction, and I didn't have to do all the work. It was the first time it felt almost comfortable. But it seems so fragile. I'm afraid tomorrow we could be right back where we were." Wendy paused and then added almost as an afterthought, "I thought this course began as well as all of my other ones have. Then you and I talked about ways to make it even better. I think part of my reaction has been to the contrast between where I imagined the class going and what has actually happened. So you see, Bob, it's partly your fault. If you hadn't helped me to see myself as a good teacher, I wouldn't feel quite so bad."

Bob heard Wendy chuckle as she said this, and he decided now, while she was in a better frame of mind, was the time to confirm his meeting with her students. "So, next Monday I'll…"

"I don't think I'm ready for you to meet with them." Bob saw that Wendy's jaw was clenched. "I want to get the class back on track first. Otherwise, it may be a waste of your time and theirs." Wendy turned away from Bob slightly and toward the stack of papers she had been grading. He had the impression she was slightly embarrassed by her refusal to let him meet with the class and was trying to end the conversation quickly.

"On the other hand, Wendy, it may be even more valuable now as you try to figure out why this class is so different." Bob was trying desperately to say something that would change her mind. He might be able to help Wendy if he could hear the students' view of the situation.

"I'm afraid it might backfire. It could make things even worse. No, I'm just not ready to go ahead. I'll think about rescheduling later in the semester. I'll call you in a couple of weeks or so." Though she was looking at him, Bob could see her body was facing the papers and her pencil was poised to go back to grading them. He wished her luck with the class and reluctantly stepped out into the hall.

As he walked back to his office, Bob wondered if he should have pushed harder to convince Wendy to let him meet with her students. He might have been able to help her discover why her students were so passive and to offer some suggestions. On the other hand, he was new to this process and was afraid that by meeting with the students he might make a difficult situation worse.

Bob thought perhaps this was a matter of Wendy's learning that classes, like individual students, have personalities, and she had gotten a class with a less than dynamic personality. But he also wondered if somewhere he had missed clues that should have helped him to anticipate this situation. Now that seemed beside the point; the urgent question was what, if anything, he could do to help Wendy.

# Assessment at Woebegone State*

*by Lesley K. Cafarelli*
The Collaboration for the Advancement of College Teaching & Learning

## ABSTRACT

A hard-working psychology professor chairs an assessment task force that attempts to please everyone: the accrediting body, the university administration, the faculty, and the members of the task force itself. The proposed assessment plan meets resistance at a number of levels, and the chair despairs of bringing people together on a solid plan.

## POSSIBLE DISCUSSION QUESTIONS

1. What are the main issues in the case?

2. What should Tony do?

---

*We acknowledge Pat Hutchings, Theodore J. Marchese, and William H. Welty for selected ideas borrowed from their 1989 case, "Assessment at Random State."

# Assessment at Woebegone State

### I. Tony's New Assignment

Tony Bush jotted down notes on his voice-mail messages, set them on the desk beside the letter from the Educational Policy Committee, and slumped back in his chair. It was only mid-November, and the first dusting of snow danced in the sun, but already he had regrets. After seventeen years at Woebegone State University, his life as professor of psychology had been satisfying and predictable. With courses from freshman through graduate levels, he enjoyed and worked hard at his teaching. His research was also stimulating, thanks in part to his two energetic undergraduate assistants.

Why on earth had he agreed to take on this assignment as chair of the university's Task Force on Student Assessment? He knew from the start, of course, that developing the university's assessment plan for the North Central Association (NCA) would be difficult; after all, the university was very complex, with its 5,500 FTE (full-time equivalent) students (including 5,000 undergraduates), three hundred faculty (including about seventy-five adjuncts and part-time faculty), three colleges (Arts and Sciences, Education, and Agriculture), and thirty departments, most of which offered both undergraduate and graduate programs. But the topic—assessing student achievement—interested him, and, given his professional curiosity about administration, he had viewed the job as an exciting intellectual challenge and a chance to test his leadership skills. He also had fifty percent released time to focus on the project.

"If you run into problems—and you will—try to come up with some possible solutions," Lucy Baldwin, the new Vice-President for Academic Affairs, had told him when he accepted the assignment. "I have every confidence in you, Tony. You are a dedicated and accomplished teacher, with a strong record of committee service—just look at your contributions to the Task Force on Student Recruitment and Retention. Even colleagues who have taken opposing positions on issues speak highly of you. Besides," she laughed, "your teaching and scholarship on motivation should stand you in good stead!"

Lucy's trust in him to pull this off meant a lot to Tony. An accomplished teacher and scholar in political science, she was the first woman vice-president and the first African-American administrator at Woebegone State. Only four months on the job, she was due to submit the university's plan to North Central by June and was under pressure from the president to implement assessment in the General Education program and in every academic major by the following fall. And these were only some of the problems left over from a year of public debate about educational quality, budget cuts, and frozen salaries.

### II. The Task Force

Lucy had also appointed the rest of the Task Force, relying on Tony, who knew the campus better, to suggest most of the other twelve members. It was a diverse group for this mainly white campus, balanced in gender, experience, and discipline and with one Asian-American woman, the director of the Student Learning Center. The other members included Fred Cunningham, director of the Center for Teaching and Learning and associate professor of education, the director of Institutional Research, and three faculty from each of the three colleges.

The Task Force had made great progress since August, Tony thought. First, they had invited two outside consultants to make presentations at the opening faculty retreat (an annual event involving all the faculty)—one on NCA's expectations and the other on the pros and cons of different assessment methods. Most of the faculty, energized by the summer break and happy to see their colleagues, seemed curious about assessment and, from the written evaluations, satisfied with the presenters.

Then, in early September, Tony had met with department chairs to help them get their faculty started on plans to assess students in the major programs. These activities were going well (especially in nursing, psychology, math, and education), he thought, even though some faculty had grumbled about the extra work and meetings just as the fall term was starting. Nevertheless, most people seemed to be engaged in the process and interested in tracking the success of their majors.

Finally, the Task Force had focused on assessing general education. Last revised eight years before, the Gen. Ed. program involved a distribution requirement to be satisfied from a slate of sixty courses across four curricular areas (Arts and Humanities, Social and Behavioral Sciences, Math and Science, and Communication), plus one of eighteen senior capstone courses specified by the major department. Although certain vocal members of the Task Force had haggled about the approach, most finally agreed on the key points, and they had sent Tony off to draft the proposal. They now had the draft and planned to discuss it at a meeting the next week. The key recommendations went as follows:

1. To assess knowledge and skills, entering students would complete the ACT-COMP, a commercially available multiple-choice test, providing a comparison with national norms.

2. To assess student perceptions, attitudes, and values, focus groups of sophomore and senior students would be interviewed in person or by interactive computer.

3. To assess the accomplishments and satisfaction of graduates, alumni surveys would be administered at five-year intervals.

4. To carry out these assessment activities, the university would establish an Office for Student Testing and Assessment under the director for Institutional Research.

Tony was confident that the Task Force had identified an efficient approach that wouldn't place too many demands on faculty time. He expected some minor revisions, but not much more.

## III. Unexpected Outcomes

So, sitting in his office, Tony was surprised by the items in front of him:

First, there was the message from Paul Anderson, chair of history, who called to schedule an appointment. "I've been talking with John Fisher in economics," he said. Well-respected faculty and department chairs, Paul and John had served with Tony on various committees, and he considered them to be like-minded colleagues and good university citizens. Both departments seemed to be making good progress on plans to assess their majors. Paul's message continued. "We've got serious questions about this business with assessing Gen. Ed. How are you going to use this info? Why do we need it, as long as we're assessing students in the major? We already know that many of our students are getting great graduate school placements. Besides, how are these interviews going to tell you anything about what they learned in Sam Hoover's Intro. to European History? He's a gruff old coot, but one of our best researchers."

The second message was from Fred Cunningham, Director of the Center for Teaching and Learning and a member of the Task Force. For two years, Fred had worked steadily to build faculty involvement in the center, which was funded by a grant and offered one-on-one teaching consultations, a resource library, and workshops on teaching methods and course development. It wasn't easy; some faculty protested that a program to improve teaching made Woebegone State look to a critical public like something was wrong. "Tony, I've read the proposal, but it's still not clear to me: How will assessment help faculty improve their teaching?" Fred questioned. "Assessment should mean more demand for faculty development; that would be great. But our grant runs out in another year. Then what? On the other hand, some people think 'assessment' is a dirty word. If the center gets involved with it, we could have more trouble recruiting faculty to participate. Call me back, will you?"

Finally, there was the letter from the Senate Educational Policy Committee, signed by Marjorie Davis, professor of English, and six other tenured faculty. Although Tony didn't know them personally, he recognized them as high-profile people, elected by the faculty in their colleges or appointed by the president to serve on key Senate Committees and special advisory groups. The letter was addressed to Lucy Baldwin and copied to the whole faculty. It read:

> The Educational Policy Committee is deeply concerned about the Task Force's proposal. We resist any plan to provide assessment data for the evaluation of individual faculty. Outside demands for accountability are motivated by political pressures and budget controls; they are a challenge to academic freedom and not in the interest of our students. Comparisons with other institutions are dangerous. Each year, our student body is changing and is less prepared academically. No assessment process can capture the quality of good teaching or the great diversity of faculty and disciplines that are the strength of this university. In the interest of safeguarding university resources, we protest any administrative action that will waste time and money on collecting meaningless data instead of spending it on serving students and retaining good faculty.

Tony let the messages sink in. His face reddened as he felt betrayed. The committee's tactics seemed unnecessarily inflammatory. Lucy must have seen the letter by now.

As though acknowledging his thoughts, the phone rang, and it was Lucy. "Tony, I'm so glad you're there! We need you to come over to President Gage's office right away. Members of the Black Student Caucus and their faculty advisors are barricading the president's office to protest the assessment plan." Her voice was strained. "And we need to talk about this Educational Policy letter. Remember, a draft of my report to the board on the plan is due to the president in three weeks."

As he hung up, Tony wondered why he was ever interested in administration.

# Is Something Rotten in Denmark?

*by Rebecca Kamm*
Northeast Iowa Community College

## ABSTRACT

Two professors, one from an American college and one from Europe, compare notes on their experiences as exchange professors. They discover that expectations, preparation, and the collegial environment can all be improved to make such exchanges successful for the participants, their students, and their academic institution.

## POSSIBLE DISCUSSION QUESTIONS

1. How could Donna and Olga have better engaged their students?

2. What are some cultural differences that might have caused difficulties between each teacher and her students?

3. Did stereotypes affect the way students and teachers felt about each other?

4. How does a teacher's relationship with her peers affect her ability to effectively handle a class?

5. How could each teacher have become better prepared for an exchange teaching position?

6. Was a language barrier a contributing factor to the problems each woman encountered?

7. How does working in another culture differ from visiting it?

8. Does teacher training in the United States adequately prepare teachers for a multi-cultural society?

9. How can teachers learn more about other cultures?

# Is Something Rotten in Denmark?

As Donna entered the faculty lounge, she caught a glimpse of Olga, a German exchange teacher at her college. Olga was sitting alone, gazing out the window. Donna detected a tear as Olga moved her hand to her face to wipe away the moisture.

Donna approached Olga, feeling guilty that she hadn't spent much time with her. However, the holidays were nearing, compositions were waiting to be graded, and committee work needed to be completed.

"Hi, Olga! It's a beautiful day!" exclaimed Donna.

"Actually, it's not," replied Olga as she cast her eyes to the floor.

"What's wrong?" asked Donna with concern.

"I don't want to sound ungrateful. People have been kind to me. The college prepared a comfortable apartment for me and has allowed me to use all the facilities here. But I'm having problems with my classes. I can't seem to get through to the students, and they don't behave as I expected."

"I'm sorry you're having a rough time," said Donna. "I was an exchange teacher a few years ago, and I had similar problems, so I know what you're going through."

"Really?" asked Olga as her eyebrows shot up with interest. "Where were you located?"

"I was at a business college in Denmark where I taught first-year students aged 16 to 20," replied Donna.

"Would you tell me about your experience?" Olga wondered.

Donna began to visualize the students in her Danish classroom and shook her head. "The students were not what I expected either. My stereotype of European students was that of sophisticated, studious, mature individuals with strong skills in the areas of languages, math, and science. Instead, students were unruly. They threw paper, ate throughout the class period, and talked constantly among themselves. Student-made signs containing vulgar language and girly pinups were taped to classroom walls. Although smoking was prohibited in classrooms, students continually smoked in the adjacent hallway and kept unlit cigarettes in their mouths during class."

"I also had stereotypes of American students," disclosed Olga. "I thought they would be eager to learn, willing to discuss current issues, and at the cutting edge of technology."

"What is your perception now?" asked Donna.

Olga finally smiled as she related, "I hope you won't take offense, but some of the students sit in the back row without saying a word. I don't know if they dislike me, are bored, or don't understand the subject material. Do they act the same way for American teachers?"

Donna was honest in her answer. "Yes, I must admit we get all kinds of students. Sometimes a classroom contains students who are eager to learn and have enough confidence to speak their minds during relevant discussions. Other students are too intimidated to say much, immature, or not prepared for the more rigorous college material."

"How did you handle the problems in your Danish classroom? Did the other teachers help you?" asked Olga.

"My Danish colleagues told me that they waited until the second year of college for students to mature. The only disciplinary actions I saw taken by teachers were to lecture students about keeping the rooms clean and sending unruly students to the college dean.

"Before arriving in Denmark, I received little direction regarding my teaching assignment even though I had contacted my counterpart several times by mail. I had no information about student profile, college policies, or curriculum. The regular teacher had supposedly already covered the main objectives of the course, and my job was to help them improve their English. My counterpart advised me that whatever I taught would be okay."

"At least I had more direction in class content," stated Olga. "The college sent me the required textbooks and college catalog. However, I've discovered that my teaching style is different from the regular teacher. I'm more used to giving factual tests, whereas these students have been writing essays and giving class presentations. They seem to blame me if they don't test well."

Donna definitely related to Olga's dilemma. "What you describe is very interesting. My attempts to promote group work didn't work well, and I later realized that students hadn't been instructed in group work techniques. I also discovered that students' sole concern seemed to be increasing skills necessary to pass the national exam in order to move to the next level. Since I wouldn't be administering the exams and possessed little knowledge of them, students didn't appear to take me too seriously."

"How did you handle assignments?" Olga inquired in a soft voice.

"My problems in this area were many," answered Donna. "Most students didn't complete homework assignments or contribute voluntarily to class discussion. Although I'm an experienced teacher who feels comfortable with all my classes at home, it was difficult for me to catch the attention of my Danish students. Students didn't respond to classroom management strategies that have been successful in my American classrooms."

"I feel the same way," added Olga with surprise. "Can you give me an example of a specific situation?"

Although several events came to mind, Donna selected the one that had perplexed her the most.

"As I walked in the doorway at the beginning of class my third day of teaching, paper airplanes whizzed in several directions. I recounted that during my years of teaching at the college level only one student had ever been immature enough to throw a paper airplane. I firmly stated that throwing paper was not acceptable and directed students to pick up garbage strewn across the floor before the lesson would begin.

"Later in the session, I saw a piece of paper being thrown to a student. I intercepted the paper and threw it away. As soon as the paper hit the garbage can, I heard the offending student call me a 'bitch' in English."

"What did you do?" asked Olga.

"I immediately took the male student in the hall where I told him that never in my life had such language been used to describe me, and I would not accept such treatment in any country. The student retorted that I had no right to take his personal property."

"What did the other teachers advise?"

"One of my colleagues spoke with the student," continued Donna. "The teacher later told me that the student didn't understand the exact connotation of the offensive word. He had heard it used in American movies and, in fact, used the same work in reference to his mother and sister. The teacher said his explanation wasn't used to excuse the boy, just to help me understand how words have varied meanings in different cultures. As a person who has seen movies where such language is used, I felt that the student must have realized the word in question would not be appropriate when addressing a teacher."

"My American students don't appear to treat me with as much respect as native teachers," related Olga, "but the circumstances vary from yours. Since English is not my first language, some students appear put off by my accent and say they can't understand me. There have been complaints that my grading is too hard, although I'm using the same system that I use in Germany."

"I assume that many of your students have never experienced a foreign teacher before," suggested Donna. "Although my Danish students all knew English, I now wonder if they were intimidated by my native command of the language."

"Did your Danish counterparts provide insights into dealing more effectively with the students?" asked Olga.

"Not really. In fact, I felt very frustrated by my colleagues' lack of interest in me. Since I didn't know a word of Danish, I was unable to read memos and school-related postings. Colleagues didn't volunteer to translate memos or inform me of special events. I introduced myself to co-workers, passed out business cards and small gifts, and initiated conversations during lunch hours. Although teachers politely answered questions, they seldom sat next to me or inquired about my comfort. They indicated they were too busy to invite me to their homes or into the community."

"I don't seem to be accepted as a professional or a friend either," said Olga. "I anticipated that as an exchange faculty member here I would be more involved in the college activities. I haven't been invited to speak to other classes or join in committee meetings. Although my colleagues are friendly at work, I haven't gained any personal friendships. I'm starting to feel as if I'm not such a good teacher after all."

Donna nodded her head in understanding. She recalled the memos announcing Olga's appointment and the reception upon her arrival. At a small college, a new teacher was quite visible, yet Donna surmised that faculty would feel Olga was doing fine unless she said otherwise.

"I definitely learned that I was totally unprepared to teach in another country," added Donna. "Instead of feeling welcomed, special, and encouraged, I felt confused, lonely, and rejected. How could we make the next exchange easier for the teacher and students?"

# Teaching Semantics:
# Euphemisms, Taboos, and Obscenities

*by Richard Betting*
Valley City State University

## ABSTRACT

This case illustrates the power of language—even when teachers and students study language itself in an attempt to understand how it influences us. Students who object to any encounter with taboo language enact a distressing dilemma for linguists: Naming the taboo invokes an emotional response that prevents scholarly examination of that kind of language.

## POSSIBLE DISCUSSION QUESTIONS

1. Why does Dr. Fisher feel vulnerable? How many issues are in play that affect his teaching and his status in the university?

2. What do you make of Dr. Fisher's approach to taboo language? Does the student have a valid complaint? Does Dean Anderson understand what Dr. Fisher is trying to do in his class?

3. This case is laden with irony, particularly the irony of Dr. Fisher's attempts to open up language as a symbol system, but failing to communicate effectively. Do you see one or more teachable moments here? Describe them.

4. Should Dean Anderson use evidence of Dr. Fisher's miscommunication in his Communication class to influence the decision on Dr. Fisher's tenure? Why or why not?

# Teaching Semantics: Euphemisms, Taboos, and Obscenities

"Good morning, Dr. Fisher," Dean Anderson said, and he asked the professor to have a chair. The Dean's huge oak desk dominated the space in the room, leaving Dr. Fisher several yards away from the administrator.

"If the weather holds, it will be nice for Thanksgiving next week," Dr. Fisher said. He wondered if the Dean wished to discuss his upcoming tenure process.

"Let's get right to the point, shall we?" the Dean responded. "When it comes to academic freedom, I'm as tolerant as anyone. We in higher education have to be open to many kinds of people, many different ideas. But when it comes to hurting our division and the university's public relations, I must draw the line."

"I must have missed something," Dr. Fisher said. "Is there a problem?"

"How could you not know there's a problem? After all, it's as obvious as any other unprofessional behavior, so you should be aware there is a problem."

Professor Fisher sat up straighter. "That may be," he said, "but I still don't know what it is. And right now I'd rather not guess." The first snowstorm of the year had blown through the night before, and he had barely made it home from his night course—Introduction to Communication—in a neighboring town. He had had to shovel the drive to get to his first class that morning. He was tired.

"Well," the Dean said, "I received a call last night from a lady who was in your Communication class. She was extremely upset by the language you used. She wanted to know if I knew what was going on in the classes in the college and if the college condoned the practice of using obscene language in class."

Dr. Fisher didn't know whether to laugh or cry. He tried a careful smile. "Well, she was referring to last night's lesson on semantics: euphemisms, taboo language, and obscenities. I try to cover them as a group because I want students to see that how we use words and how we respond to them is pretty largely socially conditioned and determined. It begins with the idea that language uses a symbol system. It's Korzybski's 'The word is not the thing' principle."

"I don't care about the principle. I want to know why you were using obscene language in class. You can't go around offending people, you know."

Dr. Fisher decided to explain and started again, in more general terms. "You see, it's part of language study to know what words mean. Words don't have meanings: meanings are in people's heads. Meanings are inside us, not out there. If we can't figure out where meanings come from, we have a hard time with all of the rest of communication."

"I understand that. But you apparently miscommunicated with her because she heard you use obscene words."

"What were they? Did you ask?"

"Yes, but she didn't want to tell me. She doesn't use that kind of language, she said." He paused. "She said you used the 'F-word,' for one thing."

"Oh, yes. I used 'fuck' and some other common taboo words to show them how language takes on emotional connotations, meanings beyond the word's referent—its denotation—beyond even the symbol itself. 'Fuck' is the best example of that because even as I discuss it in class—objectively, you know—it carries a lot of emotional baggage with it."

"The point is she was upset. You don't seem to understand."

"No, the student didn't understand. She wasn't supposed to get upset, because we were talking about language as symbols. We weren't using that language on one another. There's a huge difference." Dr. Fisher was getting emotional even as he explained. "The point is that if she was offended, she missed the entire point of the discussion. She failed to get the message."

"It seems to me you failed, perhaps, too. If you can't get the message across without offending students, then you must have failed, too. Why don't you use other words? Words like 'freezer' or 'fork' instead of the 'F-word?'"

"It's not the same. The emotional impact is gone and the point of the lesson is lost."

The Dean opened a file. "This is not the first time either. I have had student complaints before and have not made an issue of them. I gave you the benefit of the doubt, but now this language thing has become an issue."

Dr. Fisher wondered what the Dean could mean. Students had never complained to him before. But he recalled a student two years before requesting not to be required to attend the class during which he said he was going to discuss obscene language. "Why not?" he asked. "I don't use that kind of language," she said, "and I don't like to listen to it either. I don't think you can require me to attend."

So he had explained that in the class he would not be using the words in the way they were normally used in conversation. The class would be analyzing words for content and emotional meanings. The student had attended the class and said she understood. But she thought he could have gotten the point across without using the words themselves. Dr. Fisher thought otherwise. Just as he had tried to explain to Dean Anderson.

He had also tried to point out that obscene was in the minds of beholders. That many things could be obscene. War, for example. Starvation. Child abuse. Obscenity could be behavior, perhaps, not just verbal symbols, although words and pictures were what most people thought of when they heard the word "obscene." Obscene could be defined as offensive to one's taste, values, sense of propriety, as well as being lewd, Dr. Fisher explained. It was a lengthy explanation, one that, he had said, most people could not initiate with the linguistic situation in progress.

As recurring images, words, scenes came to him, Dr. Fisher snapped back to the present. "The language thing?" he said.

"Yes. It seems you have used sexist language in class too. A young lady brought this to my attention last semester. She said you talked about women's roles, feminism, and even talked about God as she."

Suddenly Dr. Fisher remembered the lecture on sexist language, in that case in a composition class. "She must have missed my introduction, my explanation. They were to avoid using sexist language unless they wished to make a point by using it. That was a lesson on appropriate use of language in context. She took the examples out of context."

Dean Anderson seemed not to hear him. He continued. "She said you used phrases like 'Women's work,' 'Women's roles are to cook, clean and sew,' and so on."

Dr. Fisher groaned. "Irony. Using examples."

"And another complaint—one that I bring to your attention cautiously because it could be very damaging—is that you have used ethnic or racially biased language in class. You talk in Black dialect I'm told. Or Norwegian. Or German. This sounds very dangerous. It's not what the public wants to hear about."

One of Dr. Fisher's communication techniques had been to use dialects in talking to students, just as he had, when he lectured, changed volume, pitch, emphasis, pronunciation, even grammar. He raised his voice. He used "ain't," "he don't got none," and the like for emphasis.

He also used examples a lot and for some of them—to keep student attention—spoke in makeshift dialects. Students had not complained. In fact, several he met after class had ended asked him if he still used those funny voices.

"I don't like to get calls complaining about my faculty. It hurts our image and in the long run may affect enrollment. You put me on the spot, " the Dean said.

"I see. What would you suggest that I could do that would make my teaching effective and not offend anyone?" Dr. Fisher said.

"Well, of course, we can't interfere with academic freedom, but I would hope you could innovatively think of ways to avoid offending students. This would certainly help your case for tenure."

Dr. Fisher blinked. After a pause, he rose, mumbled, "Good day," and aimed himself toward the door.

# Part IV:
# Cases about the Changing Culture
# As It Affects Higher Education

# Introduction

*by Carol Rutz*
University of Minnesota-Twin Cities

Educational institutions reflect the culture that supports them. As the student population becomes more inclusive, the resulting diversity of age, gender, race, ability, ethnic origin, and class both strengthens and challenges higher education. This group of cases pulls together a number of situations that focus on issues of fairness and accountability within a changing cultural context.

Nancy, the teacher of "The Cancer Student," must decide how to accommodate a student's deteriorating health while balancing her own feelings and institutional standards. At what point does respect for a student's effort conflict with the rules?

"Facing the Reality of Students' Preparation and Research Skills" involves two faculty who prepare a dynamite assignment requiring hands-on library research. Both are disappointed by the quality of students' work and their complaints about the difficulty of the assignment. Given a diverse student body, how do teachers assess preparedness and challenge students appropriately? What is "college level" work?

Faculty who do their best to adjust to students' needs can be caught between departmental standards for attendance and performance and federal rules requiring accommodation of disabilities. "Faltering Steps under the ADA" shows how business professor Dick Debit got involved in such a mess.

Authority in the classroom applies not just to making and enforcing rules, but to the teacher's qualifications in a given subject area—both in terms of knowledge and cultural perspective. For example, can an experienced white historian teach African history to African Americans? The title character of "Jalen" is a black student who challenges a white history professor's cultural perspective as a teacher of black history.

A growing segment of the post-secondary student body is made up of nontraditional students. Such a student is typically twenty-five or older, often has family and work responsibilities, and brings a wealth of nonacademic experience to the classroom.

However, there are "Special Circumstances" when a course syllabus and a professor's careful management just don't fit with a nontraditional student's many responsibilities. What obligations do teachers and students have in such situations?

Public secondary schools must deal with behavioral problems arising from student resistance to legal requirements such as regular attendance until a designated age. In some cases, this resistance is culturally based. A white school principal in a school with Native American and white students must decide how to handle a pair of persistently disruptive Ojibwe students, as seen in "They're Acting Really Squirrelly."

Even the best of intentions can go awry, as Dr. Sensee learns in "Organic Lab Is Hell." The professor's investment of extra time in a disabled student proves frustrating for both of them when the student grieves his grade. In this case, the student's ambition to become a doctor is set against his physical ability to learn what doctors have to know.

Faculty who mine the rich ore of cultural studies find many compelling ways to frame cultural influences for their students' consideration. In "Who's Learning?" Professor Susan Gardner is delighted with the connections her students make between biblical texts and their influence on American culture. But when the Israelites' conquest of the Promised Land is compared to white settlers' conquest of North America, an Ojibwe student sobs in class, grieving the treatment of her relatives. Does this visceral evidence of racism constitute education?

The last case in this section combines many of the diversity issues already touched upon: the nontraditional student, race, institutional standards, academic freedom, and reasonable accommodations to circumstances. "Dissin' the Prof" brings two strong, capable women into a power struggle. What guidelines can institutions use to resolve disputes like this?

The difficult situations in these cases will likely become more common as those in higher education learn to deal with increasing diversity on the part of students and teachers. We can hope that thoughtful solutions will also become more common.

# The Cancer Student

*by Carol Rutz*
University of Minnesota-Twin Cities

## ABSTRACT

A college senior asks her writing teacher for an incomplete. Risky cancer treatment is scheduled for the last three weeks of the student's final spring term. The teacher has to consider the student's needs, the institution's rules, and her own (the teacher's) sense of what is proper under the circumstances.

## POSSIBLE DISCUSSION QUESTIONS

1. Students present various emergencies from time to time that require teachers to make adjustments. What are the issues for the teacher in this case?

2. What advice would you give Nancy as she considers Leslie's request?

3. Nancy has tried to be utterly professional in her dealings with Leslie. Should she continue to interact with Leslie in that way?

4. Assume that Nancy is the first of her teachers Leslie approaches with a request for an incomplete. Does Nancy's decision affect the options for other instructors? Should Nancy consult with them?

5. How should Nancy deal with Leslie's disappearance from the class? Should she explain the situation to the other students? Wait for questions? Do nothing?

## The Cancer Student

After teaching a lively composition class, Nancy noticed that Leslie was waiting to talk with her, yielding her turn to other students so that she could be the last one to have Nancy's ear. As she listened to another student's question, Nancy wondered what today's request would be. A deadline extension? Clarification of the assignment? Change of topic? Or another health setback?

From the very first day, Leslie had stood out among the students in Nancy's spring term writing class for science students. For one thing, she was the only student who was bald. She wore a bandanna perched on her head, but it offered only token protection and no camouflage at all. As Nancy convened the class and asked students to introduce themselves, she wondered about Leslie and whether her baldness was due to chemotherapy. Well, that was a pretty silly thought—what else could it be in a twenty-one-year-old? Leslie didn't look like the type to shave her head as a fashion statement. Female pattern baldness is rare and seldom affects people of Leslie's age group. Obviously, Nancy thought to herself, this student had had treatment for cancer, Hodgkin's disease, or some other condition.

Glancing at the class list after the first session, Nancy had noticed that Leslie, along with one or two others, had registered for the class on a pass-fail basis. Many of the students, including Leslie, had expressed some anxiety about taking a writing class, so Nancy was not surprised that some would elect the pass-fail option. Nevertheless, she found herself wondering about Leslie's situation. Should she ask her about—well, what would she ask her? Nancy was stumped. She didn't want to be nosy. She didn't want to upset Leslie or offer her special attention. Yet she was curious.

As the class got to work on their writing projects, Leslie showed herself to be a skilled and thoughtful writer who took seriously suggestions offered by Nancy and peer reviewers. Her major, ecology, had prepared her to take a comprehensive view of natural systems that served her well as a writer. Having done quite well on her first two graded assignments, Leslie stopped at the front desk after class.

Nancy smiled. "Good job on that critique, Leslie. I was impressed with the way you rewrote the introduction."

"Thanks," grinned Leslie. "I think I'm getting the hang of this, much to my surprise. I put off this class until now because I really didn't think it would do me any good. Besides, I didn't want to put time into writing when I could take field courses."

"I can certainly understand that," Nancy replied and turned to erase the blackboard.

"Um, could I ask you something?" Leslie's tone stopped Nancy in mid-swipe. She turned, composing her face into a friendly expectant look.

"Sure."

"What does 'alopecic' mean?"

Nancy paused. "Could you spell it?"

"A-L-O-P-E-C-I-C, I think."

"Where did you run across that word? Can you give me some context?"

Leslie glanced toward the window. "I saw it on my chart when I was at my oncologist's office. I think it refers to me."

As lightly as possible, Nancy said, "It means 'bald.'"

Leslie giggled. "Oh, is that all? I thought it was something really bad! You wouldn't believe how worried I was!"

Nancy laughed with her. "It's annoying sometimes when people use technical terms instead of the common ones."

Yanking off her bandanna, Leslie agreed. "Yep. I'm certainly aware that I'm bald and it doesn't bother me. Look, my hair is even starting to grow back!"

Indeed, some downy brown fuzz covered Leslie's scalp.

Another class was beginning to file into the room. Nancy looked out into the room and back at Leslie, about to suggest that it was time to either finish their conversation or move it elsewhere. Leslie replaced her bandanna and gathered up her books. "Thanks. See you Friday."

"Right. So long."

By midterm, Leslie had spoken to Nancy after class four or five times, each time revealing more of her medical situation. Leslie had anomalous metastatic lung cancer, a disease that was nearly unknown in young adults. She had been diagnosed about a year before after months of puzzling symptoms. Though given a prognosis of only six months to live, Leslie went ahead with vigorous chemotherapy. She also went ahead with her life, taking a full load of classes and living independently with a roommate and several pets.

Now, at midterm of spring term, Leslie had gone to a prestigious oncology clinic to assess the effectiveness of the chemotherapy. The news was mixed. Though the cancer had not spread, it was still active. The new plan called for surgery to remove cancerous tissue, then biopsies of lymph and bone marrow. After all that, depending on the results, more chemotherapy was likely.

Every time Leslie approached her, Nancy did her best to listen and express concern, keeping the conversation focused on the class and how Leslie's medical appointments affected due dates and other class-related matters. Much as Nancy wanted to ask detailed questions about Leslie's disease, treatment, feelings, and so forth, she kept those questions to herself. As it happened, with each conversation, Leslie volunteered more information until Nancy well understood the seriousness of the disease in Leslie's terms. Nancy also understood why Leslie's performance was slipping.

Now here was Leslie, waiting after class until she could talk with Nancy alone. She announced that the surgery was scheduled for the seventh week of the ten-week term. Her treatment team predicted five to six days in the hospital and at least that many more recovering at home. Under the circumstances, Leslie wanted to contract for an incomplete in the course.

Listening carefully to Leslie, Nancy thought hard about her request. Making arrangements to complete the course later in the summer would be difficult; this was a workshop course that depended heavily on peer group involvement. Skip the final paper? That might insult Leslie, who had been reluctant to ask for favors. Substitute some other writing project? But Leslie and her group had already done preparatory research for the final paper. Something else? What else?

What mattered most? Institutional rules? Well, the university could easily accommodate an exception—couldn't it? Nancy's need to show compassion? Nancy had already done that, but here was a chance to do more. Leslie's need for a future that extended beyond her surgery? There was the rub. Leslie had put a great deal of energy into the course and wanted to satisfy herself that she could pass, even with the interruption of surgery. Interruption? Now there was a nasty euphemism; Leslie's life could end—a life incomplete in a sense far more significant than any incomplete in a course.

Nancy forced herself to focus on the course requirements. Had Leslie done enough work at this point to pass the class without the big final paper? Even though she had missed some classes, Leslie had a C average right now. Besides, Leslie's situation was serious. What if she didn't survive the surgery? Or what if she were too weak to do any work? How would either Leslie or the university be served by dragging this course out? Nancy's head was spinning. She had to make a decision. What was best? What made sense? What was fair?

# Facing the Reality of Students' Preparation and Research Skills

*by Deborah Petersen-Perlman and Marilyn Russell-Bogle*
University of Minnesota-Duluth

## ABSTRACT

A communications professor and a university librarian join forces to develop a challenging assignment for a first-year mass communications course. Both are disappointed by students' perception of the assignment as too demanding; they worry that students are unprepared for college-level research—and unwilling to make up the deficit by working hard.

## POSSIBLE DISCUSSION QUESTIONS

1. How could Susan and Lorraine better prepare students to complete the assignments made in this class?

2. How could the assignments be restructured to more accurately meet the students' present skill level?

3. What alternative options in assignment design could Susan and Lorraine present their students?

4. How could Lorraine better prepare library colleagues so that they could cope with the students' lack of research skills and their lack of equipment familiarity?

5. How could Lorraine and Susan model, collaboratively, the nature of the assignment?

6. What other information issues could Lorraine and Susan derive from the student and librarian remarks in order to improve the assignment?

# Facing the Reality of Students' Preparation and Research Skills

Susan opened the envelope and took out the student evaluations from last quarter's classes. The one class she most wanted to look at was her freshman level Introduction to Mass Communication class. She had come up with an exciting active learning assignment last quarter and she wanted to see how the students responded to it. She glanced at the summary sheet which identified things like "The amount of work required for this class was appropriate for the number of credits" and "Adequate help with class work was available when I needed it." The evaluation sheet also addressed students' perceptions of the teacher's knowledge of the subject matter and the teacher's efficacy as an instructor. Susan was bitterly disappointed by the numbers she saw. On a seven-point scale, Susan received averages of just over 4.2.

Susan had also solicited feedback from the students on an open-ended sheet on which she asked students to comment on what they liked best about the class. Page after page of comments identified students' unhappiness with the amount of work required for the class. While some students begrudgingly admitted they had learned from the active learning assignment, just about all of them implied that Susan was an unfair taskmistress in making this active learning assignment as extensive as it had been. Students did admit that Susan had been available for help with the assignment, and they also acknowledged her mastery of the subject matter, but they gave her poor marks on efficacy. After all that conceptualizing, planning, and development, those numbers and comments made Susan question whether it had been worth her efforts at improving the learning experience.

Susan had clear memories of being a student herself in the dark, anonymous comfort of the mass lecture class. Sitting in the back row of an auditorium with the lights dimmed and the lecturer droning on and on, it didn't matter to anyone whether she was there, nor did it matter whether she paid attention. God forbid anyone should call on her. Since then years passed, and now the shoe was on the other foot. Susan had become the professor and was faced with an anonymous mass of students who were as indifferent to her class as she had been to her mass lecture classes years ago.

As a teacher who loves what she does, Susan did not want students to have the attitude she had long ago. Susan's goal as a teacher has always been to engage her students in the material she is presenting. It is important to her to involve them in their own learning. The trick is to create an active learning environment in which students feel compelled to take responsibility for their own learning and are willing to share what they have learned with each other. Susan's class of reckoning was similar in size and setting to those she had experienced as a student.

Introduction to Mass Communication serves as one of three prerequisites for the Communication major and fulfills liberal education credit at Northeastern State University. The course is usually very large, attracting between one-hundred and thirty and two-hundred students each quarter. To accommodate a class with this many students, the university schedules it in a large lecture hall with fixed seating. The room is traditionally and rigidly laid out. It is not an environment conducive to small group interaction.

The evolution of the class had been arduous and occasionally painful for Susan. When Susan was first assigned the course, she approached it as a typical large liberal education course, requiring only that the students read the texts, come to class, and take quizzes and exams. Because this was a format familiar to many students (Susan's predecessors had all taught the course in this manner), the student evaluations were fairly good. Nevertheless, she was not satisfied with this structure.

Susan wanted to change the way this class was taught. She wanted to make the course more inclusive of the wide variety of student learning styles and interests within the class. She devised a new assignment which she hoped would meet both students' interests and their academic needs. Her goals for this assignment were multifaceted. She wanted students to consider the role of media in American social and political life and the importance of media in the democratic process. Furthermore, Susan wanted to encourage students to develop research, writing, and evaluative skills.

The project she developed required students to follow an issue of personal interest and public importance across media and across time. For example, this past fall quarter fell during a presidential campaign. She had asked students to select issues from the campaign such as "Health Care Reform," "The Economy," and "Foreign Policy." Students then sought out stories on those issues in newspapers, magazines, radio news programs, and television news. Furthermore, Susan thought it was vitally important for students to learn about alternative media presentations on those issues. In a ten-week quarter, they were asked to submit eight annotated bibliographic entries on media coverage of their selected issue.

Students could contract for a grade on this assignment. A grade of "C" merely required a bibliographic citation and a summary of the story. A grade of "B" entailed addressing questions such as "Is the information contained within the entries consistent with other information you have read/heard/seen on this topic? If not, in what ways does it differ? What position does the article/story take (does the author/reporter support the candidate's position or is s/he critical)? Is this source credible or biased? Offer evidence to support your assessment. Does this article/story attempt to be balanced, objective, or fair?" To receive an "A" students had to provide the summary, offer an assessment by way of the questions addressed in the "B" contract, and integrate analysis from class discussions into their responses.

Susan knew she needed help to introduce and facilitate the assignment. She sought out assistance from Lorraine, a teaching colleague from the library. Lorraine had come to Susan's upper division classes to discuss library strategies for research papers, and Susan thought a similar bibliographic instruction session would be helpful in this class as well. Lorraine brought handouts which summarized how to do research in the library. She produced a worksheet which demonstrated how to use computer data bases, and she offered a series of questions to facilitate the critical analysis needed for those students who chose to contract for an A or B.

Both women had invested a great deal in making the class more concrete and meaningful to students' experiences. Susan felt she owed it to Lorraine to share the evaluation numbers with her.

Susan started the conversation in a dejected manner. "I'm really disappointed by these student numbers. It's pretty clear that the students felt the class was too much work. I read over a few of the student comments from the evaluation sheets. A couple of students did have positive things to say. One student remarked that she was much more critical and skeptical of the media she used. Another student said that it was rewarding to learn about the wider array of media sources. For the most part, however, the comments were really wounding. Listen to these two:

> This assignment is for the birds. It's too demanding and I can never find
> the articles I need.

I don't have time to do this kind of assignment. It's a waste of my efforts. Doesn't she know I have other classes?"

Susan paused and then added: "And I thought the annotation assignment was such a great exercise."

"I'm so sorry. It was such a lot of work organizing that class," Lorraine briefly commiserated with Susan.

"Do you have any ideas about how we can take care of some of the problems?" Susan asked.

"Before we get to solutions, we should look at what the problems are from the library's perspective. I've been collecting student and librarian comments from this past quarter and it might be helpful to take a look at what they had to say." Lorraine pulled out a folder of the student remarks she had been saving and started to read them to Susan.

> This library never has anything I need.
>
> I don't have time to interlibrary loan that source. I need it today. It's due in an hour.

Lorraine then read off some of the comments she had heard from her colleagues in the library.

> We're too busy at the reference desk to be able to help all those students find an article. Why can't they be more self-sufficient?
>
> These students don't have adequate library skills to do this assignment.

Susan sighed. "That's quite a lot to think about. Now what do we do?"

# Faltering Steps under the Americans with Disabilities Act

*by Richard W. Metcalf*
University of South Dakota

## ABSTRACT

This case uses a generic college course setting to highlight a series of decisions confronting an instructor with ADA requirements. The cases focuses on the issues of the course syllabus, make-up examinations, and incomplete grading.

## POSSIBLE DISCUSSION QUESTIONS

1. As might be imagined, Dick's feelings toward Pat, ODS, and the whole problem swung from anger to compassion to frustration and back. Could he have handled the situation better?

2. Should he have held to the no make-up policy?

3. Did Pat meet the conditions of the syllabus?

4. Should Dick have let Pat run the meeting after the second exam rather than stepping in so quickly with a solution?

5. Was he wrong in introducing the idea of an incomplete?

6. Was the action fair to the other students?

7. Did Dick go against the role he was supposed to play in the department when he arranged to have the incomplete administered by another faculty member?

8. What part should ODS, regardless of its stated purpose, play in the conduct of a class?

9. Does a faculty member have a need to know the nature of a student's disability?

# Faltering Steps under the Americans with Disabilities Act

Dr. Dick Debit was hired to provide senior leadership for the business department at Mid-size State University (MSB). At the orientation for new faculty and staff, the school's EEO/Affirmative Action official spoke on the topic "Changes in University Responsibilities Arising from the Americans with Disabilities Act (ADA)." At the luncheon that followed, Dick was seated next to Jan Jones. Jan was the newly appointed coordinator of MSB's Office of Disability Services (ODS).

Dick was quite impressed with Jan's plans for keeping the faculty, staff, and students aware of their rights and requirements in working with (or through) her office. Dick did feel a chill though as she explained ODS's power to force compliance with its directives. This reminded him of the approach followed by another student affairs office during the Vietnam War. After the meetings, Dick incorporated many of Jan's ideas into his course syllabus. For example, he inserted the wording "Students registered with the University's Office of Disability Service are expected to notify me immediately following the first class if there are special requirements for them to complete this course."

In his job interview, Dick learned that one reason for hiring a senior faculty member was because the department had developed a history of leniency toward make-up examinations and granting of incompletes. The Dean specifically requested that Dick share his syllabus with other faculty members as a model for the school's pending reaccreditation visit. So, in addition to adding the section on ODS registrants, he highlighted two other parts—the ones stating, "Prior notice and instructor approval are both required for missed examinations" and "An incomplete is not considered to be a substitute for a poor grade."

### Living with Your Own Course Syllabus

That fall, Pat White enrolled in Dick's Intermediate class—one covered by the described syllabus. Before the first exam, Pat was at every class. However, Dick sensed a problem because of her general lack of class participation and obvious poor preparation. Since there were two other students in a similar situation, he intended to use the graded exam as a device to demonstrate the need for work outside the classroom.

Ms. White did not show up for exam one. While Dick was giving the test, she called his office and left a voice-mail message indicating she had become ill the previous afternoon and was under a doctor's care. She didn't contact him again until after the next class meeting—the one when the test was returned—but she did have a medical excuse.

Since Pat was already behind in the class and because of the "no make-up policy," having her prepare for and take an exam didn't seem like a good idea. Dick gave her a copy of the exam with the answers, accepted (with minimum discussion) the absence, and agreed to "fit" Pat's next three test scores into the average for exam one. Therefore, his course syllabus had not really been violated. But Dick had an uneasy feeling that he should have done more, or that a piece of the puzzle was missing.

### Enter Disability Services

As the class progressed toward exam two, Pat's attendance (and attentiveness) waned. She even missed the class just before the second test—the one where the "study hints" are supplied. When Dick returned from this review session, there was a new person on his voice mail. It was Jan, from ODS, making an appeal that Pat—who was receiving treatment under ODS direction—be excused from exam two. Jan's tone made it sound more like a demand than a request.

Pat's connection with ODS was new information—so much for the words in his syllabus about letting him know about ODS needs after the first class. Dick was not in a good mood as he returned Jan's call. On the other end of the phone, Jan was in a panic because ODS had worked for over a month to get Pat a session with a regional specialist. Unfortunately, the appointment was set for the same day and time as his exam. Rather than demanding, Jan was pleading for anything, even a make-up exam, to let Pat receive the scheduled treatment. Dick's resolve faded and he agreed, stipulating that it was up to Pat to work out the details.

Pat was even scarcer than before. She left a typed, unsigned message in Dick's mail box. This was the first of three messages he was to receive from Pat and he never learned why they were unsigned or always typed. This note indicated that she planned to take the make-up exam two hours after the one scheduled for the class. It left no room for delays in her appointment or time to become composed for the test. Dick called Pat and recommended that the make-up be put off to permit some elapsed time after the appointment. He also arranged to mail her a copy of the review outline and she reset the make-up for a time that fit her schedule.

Unfortunately, Pat still missed the make-up and the next class meeting as well—the one when the graded exam was returned to the class. Pat, by now a mystery person, left another phone message. This one requested a meeting the next day. Interestingly, the time of the message coincided with Dick's class—reinforcing the feeling that he was being avoided.

## A Chance for a New Start

Pat arrived early for the appointment—seemingly prepared to provide a complete description of her problem. Dick stopped her before she could begin her medical diagnosis. He had already called ODS, after receiving her request for a meeting, and Jan was so mysterious about Pat's problem and how he should approach her that he wasn't sure he should get involved. Besides, it might impact—either for or against—the way he evaluated her classroom performance.

Rather than having Pat prepare for a make-up exam, Dick offered her the opportunity to complete the remaining sixty percent of the class, receive an incomplete, and take an examination covering the first two sections. The test was to be taken between semesters, after allowing up to a month for review. She immediately accepted the offer and expressed great appreciation for the proposed solution. This concession was developed because of Dick's feeling that there needs to be mutual empathy (student for instructor and faculty member for the student) for maximum learning to be achieved.

Pat worked diligently in preparing for exam three. She solved extra problems and asked for frequent clarification of the material—both in class and during office hours. On examination day, she mentioned she was having problems with her new medications and her results, while adequate, were far worse than had been expected.

### Reenter the ODS

Exam three marked Pat's last day in class. However, she did leave another unsigned appeal in Dick's mail box. Her note asked for: (1) the previously offered incomplete in the course and (2) Dr. Debit to contact the ODS Coordinator for her recommendation. When Dick called Jan, she repeated Pat's request that an incomplete be granted, with the course to be repeated next semester, if possible. Since Dick was not teaching the course in the spring, this posed a problem.

Dick made arrangements with the spring semester's principal instructor to administer the course and to let the grade substitute for the incomplete. He then sent separate letters to Pat—at her campus address—and to Jan. The parallel letters said that no action would be taken on the incomplete unless ODS either sent a memo recommending the incomplete or co-signed Pat's form requesting the incomplete. Pat's letter made it her responsibility to obtain and complete the standard University form one to be signed by both student and faculty member—setting forth the conditions for removal of the incomplete grade. At this point, Dick wanted something on the record to explain the concessions being made.

Both letters set the date grades were due as the absolute deadline for their action. Dick intended to attach a copy of Jan's letter (or memo) to the incomplete form in submitting final grades to the registrar. In all honesty, Dick did not expect the deadline to be met. Lo and behold, Pat slid the requested documents under Dick's office door on the designated day and an Incomplete was granted.

# Jalen

*by Eugene Hermitte and Phyllis Worthy Dawkins*
Johnson C. Smith University

## ABSTRACT

In this case, a white professor encounters difficulties teaching African subject matter to African-American students. An African-American professor observes the class, interviews students, and presents her reflections to the professor.

## POSSIBLE DISCUSSION QUESTIONS

1. Jalen perceives this to be a problem of a white professor bringing his biases into the classroom. Does this seem to be the case?

2. How does and how should Leon respond to the challenge Jalen presents in the classroom?

3. Leon, Delores, and Jalen appear to have very different perceptions of how well the class went. Why might that be?

4. How should Delores try to help Leon? What might some of Leon's defensive points be?

# Jalen

Dr. Leon Cattani, a white professor of African history at a small, traditionally black college, leaned back from his course syllabus and reflected on the upcoming class. Though he was trying hard not to admit it, he felt nervous: Dr. Delores Finely, an African-American colleague and his peer collaborator in the Five Points College's faculty development program, was scheduled to visit his class.

Though both of them had joked with each other about the tensions of peer observation, Leon knew that he did not want to embarrass himself by performing badly in front of a colleague—especially Delores, a respected teacher. To make matters worse, they had agreed that the class would be videotaped and Delores would conduct some interviews with students to glean their reflections on the class session. Leon took a deep breath. Yes, it would be a tough class, with the camera focusing in on him from the back of the room, Delores sitting to one side writing notes, and every student looking like an investigative reporter soaking up the impressions for an interview.

There was also the fact that this class, Introduction to Africa, had several bright, articulate, idealistic, and outspoken students, and Leon was not at all sure what they would say about his teaching. Nevertheless, he and Delores had decided to ask three of the strongest students, Jalen, Malia, and David, if they would be willing to be interviewed by Delores.

The fact that Leon was white and all of the students in the class were African American with strong Afrocentric views did not particularly bother him. His field of training was African history, and he had taught at this historically black college for over twenty years, enjoying classroom discussions. Although there were some students who initially viewed the discussions and content with suspicion because he was a white professor teaching an African history course, the problems generally resolved themselves later in the term.

Leon explained Delores' presence in the class, their desire to interview students after class, and their intention to show the video of the class and the interview to faculty as part of the kick-off of a peer coaching program. The students accepted the situation without question, and the class proceeded.

The class traditionally started with a news report selected and presented by a student. Today it was about a racist memo stereotyping Africans that had circulated at a major corporation. The memo built upon the topic covered during the previous class session: myths about Africa. There was an intense discussion—almost a debate—between students about how to respond to such a situation. Malia talked about the possibility of African Americans as a block shifting their business to a rival corporation in order to pressure the offending corporation to change its behavior. She did not believe the attitude of persons in the corporation toward African Americans would change, but she thought that the corporation could be pressured into changing its image of African Americans in its advertisements.

Following Malia's position was a discussion about whether it would be better to organize separate African-American businesses, rather than attempting to influence white-dominated institutions. The discussion also turned to political possibilities and limitations, and African-American leadership.

Everything was going smoothly until a discussion between Leon and one of the students chosen for the interview, Jalen, began over "who should choose African-American leaders" to handle a problem in the African-American community. Delores wanted to jump into the discussion, but restrained herself and observed the reactions of other class members, as Leon and Jalen debated the issue. A direct confrontation occurred when a student asked, "Were there any responses to the issue from black leaders?" A student presenter responded by naming a well-known African-American leader, but several members of the class laughed when the name was given. The student presenter went on to state that leaders of other well-known African-American organizations had also responded in some fashion.

Leon challenged the leadership question by asking the class, "Could prominent spokespersons bring about some change? How would a company respond to the complaints of a nationally accepted black leader who was not necessarily black-accepted? Would that bring about a change or response?"

Jalen responded: "Is that the key—nationally accepted black leaders? Who are you talking about?"

Leon: "Look at the entire country—especially whites. If you ask them to name black spokespersons, they think of the person you just laughed at."

Jalen: "So, whites are picking our leaders again?"

Leon: "Well...in a sense." (The class laughed.)

Jalen: "We do not have true leadership if someone else is picking our leaders." With passion, Jalen repeated his statement.

Leon: "I don't want to get into whether those leaders have support from African Americans or not, but they are generally recognized by whites as being leaders. That's a different issue."

Jalen: "So, are you saying that African Americans are not leaders until whites recognize them as such?"

Leon: "No, I'm asking—who has the impact to change the problems or myths like racial stereotyping? A person with prominence in the public eye might be able to deal with this problem. We are going to have to cut off this discussion in about two or three minutes because I have other things to cover."

Jalen jumped in to let Leon know that he was not attacking him. Leon said he understood and that he wanted Jalen to say the things he felt about the topic.

Jalen continued the discussion by speaking of hand-picked, Uncle Tom-type leaders. Leon said that he was not necessarily talking about leaders, but about people who were effective spokespersons from the point of view of white society.

Delores thought that both discussants were determined to maintain their views. Whenever Jalen explained his side, some of the students in the class signified their agreement with him by nodding their heads. When Leon explained his side, the students looked intent and, at times, laughed.

The remainder of the class period was devoted to a slide presentation and a discussion about African geography. It went smoothly and much more quietly than the discussion about the news report. At the end of class, Leon exited while Delores began her interview with the three students.

Leon felt relieved. He had not been as nervous as he had expected, and he thought the exchange with Jalen had been a constructive experience. But this feeling changed dramatically when Delores emerged from the interview and told him ominously, as she was rushing to her next class, "You had a lot of courage to go through with this observation and interview, as you'll see from the video."

Leon later watched the video, which at first appeared as he remembered it. The exchange with Jalen seemed fine, although he thought Jalen initially either twisted or did not understand his comments. Later, it seemed that Jalen accepted what he was saying, perhaps because he made himself clearer by restating his meaning several times.

Leon was shocked, however, when he saw the interview portion of the video. Jalen said, "Dr. Cattani didn't realize what he was saying when he stated that leadership was not accepted until whites accept it. I cannot accept this mentality." Leon thought to himself, "I had simply been trying to state an unfortunate 'fact' of African-American politics that black leaders can not bring about much change unless they can influence the white-dominated power structure."

Meanwhile, back in her office, Delores was thinking about the classroom observation and the videotape. She concluded that she had walked into a hot topic beyond the pedagogical issues of a course and the peer coaching program. Due to the nature of the course, issues came about during the classroom observation and interview that she had not expected. Her goal was to provide Leon with feedback on issues such as teaching styles and methods of presenting course content, and to observe student responses to the information presented. She did obtain that type of information, but she also received much more.

During the student interviews, she had not responded to or elaborated on the racial issues as they surfaced, mainly because she was trying to stay focused on the pedagogical questions that were pre-selected for the interview. Also, Jalen had merely followed up on the previous classroom debate. He had also added the issue of a white professor teaching an African course because he felt comfortable with her since they were both African American. Now, as Leon's peer collaborator, she knew that she would have to address the issue of white instructors teaching African or African-American subject matter. She went to the computer and began to write.

As Delores was sitting in her office reflecting on what she had just written, Leon entered her office with a look of agitation on his face. "Delores, what happened? I need advice about what Jalen had to say."

"Calm down, Leon, and tell me what you are upset about." Leon explained, "Jalen never seemed to understand the point I was trying to make. He seemed obsessed with the idea that whites believe they must control black leadership, and that I am just another white person who believes that. How did I fail to communicate?"

# Special Circumstances

*by Jeannine L. Saabye*
University of Mary

## ABSTRACT

Despite a professor's careful course planning and ample notification, a student has an unavoidable conflict on two important class days. The teacher and student must work together on what seems to be an insoluble problem.

## POSSIBLE DISCUSSION QUESTIONS

1. When a professor plans a course, is s/he obligated to anticipate complications in students' lives that may affect the class?

2. When students present stories of special circumstances that will keep them out of class or prevent their completing class work, how can a professor decide what circumstances are indeed "special"?

3. What special arrangements have students asked you for? What special arrangement have you made and why?

4. What suggestions do you have for the professor and student in this situation?

# Special Circumstances

Anne Smith had really worked hard revising her Anthropology 301 course, and, for the most part, things had gone smoothly over the semester. She was especially pleased that most of the student work groups had jelled pretty well.

Next week—the home stretch—final projects were to begin, which required one-hundred percent attendance on Thursday and Friday. Smith had gone carefully through the university calendar to be sure that the days she selected did not conflict with any events that could pull students out of class. She had reminded students that the processes and activities that they would pursue those days were very important and represented twenty percent of their grade.

Now it was Friday, and standing at the podium she again reviewed with the class what was to happen in the coming week.

"Any questions?" she asked, stepping around the podium and down the aisle into the first row of seats.

No hands went up. She backed up and then paced a bit to the left and then to the right, trying to provide enough time for any student to ask any question. She leaned back against the desk.

No questions. No hands anyway. She glanced at the clock. Five minutes to the end of the hour. Students were starting to stuff books into their bags and slip on their jackets.

"Okay then, I'll see you on Monday, and on Thursday we'll be all ready to work in groups and tackle the final project."

Smith started to put her own things in order. She slid her lecture notes over the rings in her binder and popped it shut, closed the textbook, and turned to erase the board.

John Schmidt got up from his seat as he finished putting his notebook into his bag. He pulled out his weekly planner. He had been absent on Wednesday and somehow had also missed class the day expectations for final projects were first laid out. Now he quietly cursed the members of his group who never said a thing about projects the day he missed class because of a track meet. He wondered how come Smith had waited until now to review and lay out expectations for the coming week. His three-year-old was scheduled for a tonsillectomy next Thursday. That meant he'd miss both Thursday and Friday for sure. Monday, too, if Jason wasn't well enough to go to daycare.

He didn't really like missing class either, but with extra-curriculars (which helped him maintain his scholarship), an almost full-time job and a preschooler, what was he to do?

His wife found it impossible to get time off from her job. Now he was going to have to tell Smith. Something had to give. Why was he always about a step behind himself?

He walked up to the board.

"Dr. Smith?"

"Yes, John, what's up?" Smith turned from the chalkboard and rubbed the remaining chalk from her fingers.

"Well, I don't know quite how to say this, but I can't be in class on Thursday or Friday of next week."

"And why is that?"

"My son is having his tonsils out on Thursday. It was the only time they could schedule it and I didn't think we were doing that much in class next week."

"That's too bad. Did you have a class schedule that I handed out with the syllabus at the beginning of the semester?"

"Yes I did, but I didn't know how important this was. No one in my group told me. My wife can't get off to be at the hospital."

"Did you ask your group about what was coming up?"

"Yes, I did."

"You've been absent quite a bit, haven't you, John? At least it seems to me that you've missed quite a bit."

"Well, I couldn't help the week of music tour, or the track meets, or for that matter the two times for Nursing 201. I've only been sick a couple of times, but my kid's been sick a lot, they think because of the tonsils. It isn't that I want to miss class."

"No, I don't suppose you do, but I don't plan to change what's to be done in view of the fact that expectations for these projects were explained both in class and in the syllabus. Success is dependent on collaborative group work. How do you think this problem can be solved?"

# They're Acting Really Squirrelly

*by Thomas D. Peacock*
University of Minnesota-Duluth

## ABSTRACT

In this case (designed for use in secondary education teacher-training programs), Dale, a school principal in northern Wisconsin, must decide how to handle a pair of disruptive students. The school is a mix of Ojibwa and white students, but both of the disruptive students are Ojibwa. This case raises issues for new teachers about dealing with student diversity and behavior.

## POSSIBLE DISCUSSION QUESTIONS

1. How were Molly and Beverly behaving, and why?

2. How did the school's administrators react to the girls, and why?

3. Dale's actions result in a possible lawsuit against the school. Could he have prevented that outcome? Should he have?

4. The girls are Ojibwa. Does that seem to play a part in their behavior? In the behavior of the administrators?

5. What role do expectations for the girls seem to play in this narrative?

# They're Acting Really Squirrelly

Dale had been the school's principal for just over three years. Depending upon the situation, time of day, day of the week, or time of the year, he felt like he'd been there for thirty years. It was a decent enough school, Cross Lake Secondary High, located in the lakes and woods country of northern Wisconsin. The district of Cross Lake served just over eight hundred students, three hundred thirty-five of them attending the grades 7-12 secondary school. And, Cross Lake was a decent enough community of 1,006 souls, a community that survived when other communities had failed because it had a thriving lumber mill and good summer tourist trade. It survived also because of the growing economic influence and government jobs brought in by the Forest County Ojibwa Reservation, which bordered the primarily white community of Cross Lake.

The school's student body was a reflection of the community. The students were a nearly even mix of Ojibwa and whites, with the Ojibwa student population growing every year and the number of white students declining as families moved south to Madison and Milwaukee for better jobs. Each school year, Dale noted an increase in Ojibwa students, as the Forest County Tribal Council (FCTC) added housing complexes and business enterprises such as a restaurant/gas station complex and a bowling alley. Recently, the tribe had one of its members named to the Board of Directors of the Cross Lake Citizens Bank (a first), and a local Ojibwa (and Cross Lake High graduate) became the town's first Indian police officer. These and other signs indicated to Dale the growing influence of the tribe, accompanied by the growing uneasiness of the town's aging white power structure, one of whom had been overheard at a local cafe complaining that it "won't be too long now before them Indians take over everything."

For the most part, the Ojibwa students seemed to be very much like the white students Dale encountered on a daily basis. They seemed like typical secondary students. There were Ojibwa and white jocks and cheerleaders, Ojibwa and white druggies, and Ojibwa and white nerds. Some of the Ojibwa students were heavily involved in school activities, with one student in particular, Joe Schmitt, recently elected president of the student council. Others were the shadow side of the Joe Schmitts of the world, particularly a group of junior high Ojibwa girls led by Molly and Beverly. Molly and Beverly kept Dale busy by continually skipping school and classes, being disruptive when in classes, and conducting a reign of terror on other junior high students.

Dale usually had to call Molly and Beverly into his office three or four times a week. He made a point of doing it every morning during first period after reviewing the teachers' disciplinary referrals and drawing up a list of names for Milly, the hall monitor, to retrieve for conferences. Because Molly and Beverly were in the same section of 8th grade, they always appeared in his office in tandem.

"Here are your little darlings," Milly bellowed as she shooed the pair into his office. "Do you want me to stick around in case you give them a day in ISS (in-school suspension) and they need an escort up there, or should I go and fetch you the rest of the list?"

Dale motioned the pair to have a chair and indicated to Milly that she should stay.

"It seems Mr. Leap saw you two hiding in the laundromat on his way to the bank yesterday during 7th period. Aren't you two suppose to be in phy. ed.—or was phy. ed. held at the laundromat?"

Beverly laughed. She always laughed. Molly looked at Dale with her patented sneer, one she must have practiced every day in the mirror, because it combined elements of surprise, disdain, and humor.

"We ain't going to that Miss Krupp's class, because she's a b——," said Beverly. "And we ain't wearing them gym clothes she tries to get us to wear. She's a queer too. Always looking at us in the locker room. She just stares at us."

Milly shot a look at Beverly and said, "You watch your mouth and be more respectful. I should take you in the bathroom and wash out your mouth with soap." Milly always said that to Beverly or Molly. She never followed through with it and never would.

In his three years at Cross Lake, Dale had heard everything at least twice and very few things ever shocked him. He finished chewing on a pen and looked over toward the pair saying, "You two don't have any business in the laundromat during the school day. Whether you like it or not, phy. ed. is a required class. If you don't like the gym clothes Miss Krupp has to offer you, bring your own. I don't know what to say about her staring at you. No one else ever complains about her that way." He turned to Milly, "Take these two up to ISS for the day."

As she was being led out of the room, Molly mumbled something under her breath about not "sitting in the f——' room all day." Beverly laughed and offered her wrists to Milly as a gesture that indicated it was time for her to be cuffed and escorted to serve her time. Dale looked out the window at the approach of winter. It was only October.

He spent the rest of first period completing his list of discipline referrals. On a typical morning there were five to ten referrals, and most of the students he had seen many times in his three years as principal.

At about 11.00 a.m., Bob Moyority, the school's ISS supervisor, buzzed him on the intercom. "Those two lovelies you sent me this morning aren't going to last up here today. They'll either walk, or I'll make them walk. You'd better come up here. They're acting really squirrely."

Dale took the slow climb up the stairs to the ISS rooms, which were windowless cubicles located off the old band room. At one time they were a series of three practice rooms but had been converted for use as ISS rooms after a decline in the number of students joining band or chorus and an increase in discipline problems. He opened the door and approached Moyority, who was helping a student with an assignment. Moyority motioned him outside the door, warning the five students in the room to "keep their flippers to themselves" and not to leave their seats. They knew if they were sent from ISS it was an automatic three-day suspension from school, and most of them didn't want that.

"I think Molly and Beverly are on something. They've been giggling constantly since they came up here. I keep warning them to be quiet, but they just won't quit. I think they should be sent home. It's like they're high on something. They sure as hell aren't going to last in here."

"We ain't high," shouted Beverly, who had been poking her head out of the ISS door. "You're full of s——, Molar Teeth!" referring to Moyority with the name students only called him behind his back. "Let's get out of here, Molly." Beverly motioned to Molly, and they both walked out the door, down the stairs, and out of the building.

Dale sighed and walked down the stairs to his office. He tried to call Beverly's mother, but got a disconnected number message. He called the Indian social worker aide, who officed out of the elementary school, and left a message asking if she could go to Beverly's home and inform her mother about what had happened. He was able to reach Molly's mother at work and told her that Molly had walked out of the ISS room. "It's an automatic three-day suspension from school. I'll send you the paperwork by certified mail." Molly's mother issued a sigh of resignation and said something about not knowing what to do with the girl.

He didn't see or hear from either Molly or Beverly for the rest of the morning and figured they might be seen during noon recess by the rest of the kids on their way to the stores of downtown Cross Lake. When he checked his best informants after lunch, none recalled seeing either of the girls in town during lunch period.

At the beginning of 7th period, Dale took his customary walk through the halls as he did at the beginning of every period. He came upon Milly, the hall monitor, who chided him about the school day being "too quiet without those two lovelies." He poked his head into the ISS room, where Moyority was reading *Sports Illustrated*. The three remaining students, who had long finished their school work, were asleep with their heads upon their desks. Numerous graduate summer session lectures about time on task and teachable moments ran through his head. He sighed, shook his head slightly in disgust, and closed the door.

He returned to his office and looked out the window toward downtown Cross Lake and the town laundromat. There on the street corner in front of the laundromat, smoking cigarettes, were Molly and Beverly. They each smiled and waved at him, and he waved back. With that formality completed, they put their cigarettes out on the sidewalk and walked into the laundromat. Later, he saw them get on the school bus with the rest of the students. He didn't try to intercept them. It had been a long day.

The next day, he came to work as usual and began compiling his morning hit list of disciplinary referrals. In the pile of referrals and mail was a phone message from his secretary which read: "Mrs. Whitehorse called, and she was quite angry. She said the school suspended Beverly because she was high on drugs. She wants to know why no one bothered to get in touch with her about this. Furthermore, she took her daughter to the public health clinic after Beverly had come home and complained about being falsely accused of being on drugs. She says the doctor found no trace of drugs in her and that she was going to see Indian legal assistance about this."

Dale looked out the window of his office. It was one of those grey October mornings in northern Wisconsin, and the cold wind was pushing leaves against the corners of curbs and old brick buildings that collectively called itself downtown Cross Lake. Overhead, a flock of geese was making its way south.

"Take me with you," he whispered. "Take me with you."

# Organic Lab Is Hell

*by Elva Mae Nicholson and Marie C. Milletti*
Eastern Michigan University

## ABSTRACT

A dedicated chemistry professor devotes a great deal of time to a disabled student, only to have the student grieve his grade. At issue are the student's abilities, the professor's investment of time, energy, and emotion, and the institution's experimentation with disability accommodations. How are accommodation and disability related?

## POSSIBLE DISCUSSION QUESTIONS

1. How do you determine if a student has a physical or mental disability? Which people and resources are available on campus to help determine a student's disability and to provide the necessary support?

2. How can an instructor accommodate the needs of a handicapped student and also ensure that the student is held to the same standards as the rest of the class?

3. What is the impact on the class as a whole when a handicapped student requires extra time and effort from the instructor? How do you prevent teacher burnout in a situation such as this?

4. Should we consider students with certain types of physical and mental handicaps, such as blindness or schizophrenia, too much of a risk in a lab situation for the institution to tolerate? If so, how can we make sure that the student is not precluded access to certain careers, such as those in the health fields, because he or she could not have access to the lab?

5. What would you have done differently in Dr. Sensee's place? Do you think he should have done more for Shawn, or less?

6. Do you think it was appropriate for Dr. Sensee to discuss Shawn's problems with other instructors? At which point, if any, should the department head have been told of Shawn's problem?

7. Why do you think Shawn wanted to grieve his grades? What do you think Shawn would have wanted the Department and Dr. Sensee to do about his special situation?

# Organic Lab Is Hell

"Damn, that lab wears me out," I complained to my colleague Peter while gulping a cup of coffee.

"But you have only six students and that's really light. I had eighteen students in that lab last semester—now that's rough," responded Peter, never known for his sympathy. "You must be over the hill."

"Yeah, I guess. It's that one student Shawn. I spend more time with him than everyone else combined. He is the slowest student I've ever had. It's so damn frustrating. I go over the difficult parts of the experiment with the group, then I go over them with him again and he still screws up. I swear he just doesn't listen. He no more than turns around when he's forgotten what we just went over. He's really a nice guy, but I'm losing my patience. He gets these horrible products and his grades certainly show it. But he's always pleasant when he turns in his little bit of brown gum while everyone has nice white crystals."

Peter was shaking his head. "Sounds like he's student of the year. Let's go get lunch."

"I can't. Shawn's coming to see me in half an hour. He really blew the first test. No surprise there. But he wants to talk about it with me."

"Egads—he's in your lecture too. A double dose. Better you than me. See you later," commented Peter, again not helping me feel at all better.

Even my peanut butter and anchovy sandwich couldn't raise my spirits as I awaited Shawn's arrival. "I must be a glutton for punishment meeting him so soon after lab," I thought. "Maybe a couple of aspirins will help my head. I'm known for my patience, but even Mother Teresa couldn't deal with this guy. Calm down—remember tennis with Ed at 4:30 to look forward to. I can bash the ball to my heart's content. The way the day is going, it will rain or even snow by then."

My reverie was interrupted by Shawn's knock on the door. "Dr. Sensee, may I come in?" As I waved him to a chair in my cluttered office, I considered what a clean-cut, well-spoken and polite young man he was. "I wanted to talk to you about my test. You see, I'm a premed and I have to do well in this class." I got ready for my usual "How many hours a day are you studying?" and "Do you do the problems?" questions that usually arise in such a discussion. Instead Shawn continued. "I don't want you to think I'm not studying. It's just that I need more time on the exam. I have this problem." He hesitated, his eyes dropping to the floor.

"Please sit down," I encouraged. "Do you want to tell me about it?"

"I have a problem. I need more time," he blurted out, looking down at the floor.

He sounded so frustrated that I held back on my usual commentary about how all students feel that way about organic tests and instead suggested, "Sit down, Shawn. Let's talk about it."

"I study, honest I do. I just can't always think right. Everything now takes so long. I used to do well. It's so unbelievably frustrating!" The words gushed forth "It's been almost two years since my accident. This truck went through a red light and hit my Escort broadside. My head held up the roof. They tell me I had to be pried out of the car. A week later I come to, a miracle they say—but they don't live with this day to day. Seizures, blackouts, memory loss—some miracle."

"That's really rough, Shawn," I interjected when he paused. I felt like an insensitive jerk for having been impatient with him, for all the times I had told him he had to pay attention to what he was doing. "If you think that having more time on the test would help, that can be arranged easily."

"Sometimes it just helps not to have pressure. I would appreciate the extra time," he answered, looking more relaxed.

So I arranged to give Shawn all the time he needed on the second test and sure enough, his grade improved...to a D. But at least it was a passing grade. On the other hand, in the lab things went from bad to worse. Despite all my efforts, his results continued to be atrocious. As the semester went on, Shawn fell further and further behind, even though I stayed overtime with him in the lab virtually every day. I went out of my way to give him all sorts of detailed instructions and I treated him with all the patience I could muster, but nothing helped, since his short-term memory seemed nonexistent.

After a while, I tried writing down instructions for him to follow so that he could refer to them as often as he wanted. But as soon as I started tending to another student's questions, Shawn was following me around with more problems. Unless I was standing over his shoulder and repeating instructions one by one, he would make errors. In desperation, I resorted to performing entire laboratory procedures for him, so that he could get some sorts of results. I didn't think that he was learning anything. He would know no more when he was finished than if he had never been there at all.

"I am spending incredible amounts of time with Shawn. If it were making a difference, I wouldn't mind so much, but he's not learning anything. So I'm feeling used up," I exhaustedly told my colleague Mary, well known for her incisive analysis as well as her empathy.

"Sounds like he doesn't belong in the lab. What if he has an accident and gets injured, or one of the other students is injured?" Mary questioned. "I wonder if the legal system would consider us more at fault for allowing him to remain in the lab knowing he's incompetent or for dropping him from the lab because he has a disability. The details of the new Disability Act remain to be tested in the courts. Seems like we could have trouble either way."

"I think you're right. What a bind! Right now I'm just workingt for the end of the semester."

"Is he going to pass?" Mary inquired.

"He's got a chance for a D in lecture—I don't see how he can pass lab unless I just hold my nose and give him a D-. I'll really consider that."

## Postscript

Shawn got his D in Organic Chemistry lecture and Dr. Sensee breathed deeply and granted him a D- in the lab.

A few days into the next semester, the chemistry department head received a letter from Shawn, wanting to file a grade grievance about his lab grade. In his perception, Dr. Sensee had spent all his time with the women in the class and he discriminated against him because he was a male.

# Who's Learning?

*by Beverly J. Stratton*
Augsburg College

## ABSTRACT

Well-crafted assignments with worthy goals can sometimes evoke surprising reactions from students. In this case, an assignment that connects the Bible's influence on American culture upsets a Native American student and leaves the professor questioning her own motives.

## POSSIBLE DISCUSSION QUESTIONS

1. Susan clearly regrets the pain that Linda felt. Is Susan to blame for Linda's feelings? Why or why not?

2. How do you predict students will deal with this incident in their journals?

3. If you were Christine, how would you advise Susan as she evaluates her series of assignments?

4. Has one of your assignments evoked a surprising reaction from students? If so, what was the issue and how did you address it?

# Who's Learning?

Susan Gardner loved teaching the introductory cultural studies course. No matter how often she used her favorite assignments, the material was never stale or dull for her, and students seemed to really dig into the issues she raised for their consideration.

This week, students were to present group projects that demonstrate the influence of the Bible on American culture. The Monday classes had done an excellent job of staging slavery debates. They chose up sides as American Christians from the 1850s and argued pro- and anti-slavery positions on the basis of the Bible.

One student actually stood on a box with "SOAP" written on it in crayon and intoned, "We have an obligation to care for these poor unfortunate beings who were ripped from their primitive jungle lives. It is our Christian duty to bring them to the Lord, nourishing them spiritually as well as providing for their physical needs. They are clearly incapable of caring for themselves in our world. We neglect them at the peril of our own immortal souls."

This appeal was answered by an anti-slavery orator, who accused her peers of "violating God's will by subjecting his creatures to the same violent, outrageous treatment that Pharaoh forced upon the Israelites during their Egyptian captivity."

Susan enjoyed the discussion which revealed how context affects interpretation. Students demonstrated skillfully that the "good book" could easily be used to back very different positions on slavery.

At the next class, on Wednesday, the insights from the slavery debate helped students interpret a novel by Zora Neale Hurston that retold the Exodus story. More than one student began to understand the power of the narrative cycle: captivity-promise-deliverance-disobedience-renewed promise-redemption.

Susan was exhilarated. "I'm so glad I developed these assignments," she thought on her way back to her office Wednesday afternoon. "I really want to tell Christine about them during our mentoring session on Friday. She may want to adapt them for one of her courses—the issues are incredibly rich."

As she expected, the first section on Friday went as well as all of her classes during this wonderful week. Feeling on a roll, she eagerly awaited the arrival of the second section.

Students filed into the room with the usual amount of chatter and found seats near their group members. The source material for today's group was an article by Native American author Robert Allen Warrior, called "Canaanites, Cowboys, and Indians." The presenting students were Linda, Martin, and Jennifer. They whispered among themselves for a moment. Then Linda, the leader, cleared her throat and began.

"Martin is going to summarize the Warrior article. Jennifer and I will analyze the ways that Warrior uses cultural material from the Bible to make his points."

Martin began. "Basically, Warrior warns American Indians against climbing too quickly on the liberation theology bandwagon. He notes that Israel entered its promised land by defeating the Canaanite nations who were already in the land—and the Israelites do this because of God's command to 'utterly destroy' these nations. Warrior points out parallels to Europeans and how they slaughtered inhabitants of the Americas because they saw themselves entering a place they thought was their promised land. Finally, he reminds us that not all the stories are told: the Canaanites aren't heard in the Bible."

Martin paused for questions. Susan glanced around the room, hoping students would have comments. Then she noticed that Linda, the group leader, had tears in her eyes and was covering her mouth with her hand. Her eyes briefly met Susan's, and Linda could no longer hold back her emotion. To everyone's surprise, Linda sobbed and sobbed, while the whole class tried to become invisible.

Susan was about to guide her out of the room when Linda seemed to pull herself together. "I'm so sorry," she gasped. "But this stuff brings back too many sad stories. Too many unhappy memories. You see, I'm Ojibwe."

The whole class inhaled. And stopped breathing.

Susan recovered first. "Linda, I didn't realize that your heritage would be at issue in this assignment. I—"

Linda wouldn't let her finish. "Don't worry about that, Dr. Gardner. I thought I could handle it. But hearing Martin talk about the article and the way the Canaanites suffered—supposedly according to God's will—it all made me feel so bad about my grandmother. Her family was so frightened that she would be destroyed or abused by whites that they sent her away to a boarding school for Indians. Out of fear, they took her family away from her, and she had to make her own way with other rejected children and really mean teachers. And that's nothing compared to the lousy things that happened to other Native Americans. The U.S. government was really thorough—they used guns, horses, soldiers, and the Bible to almost obliterate my people, my culture." At this, Linda lost it again.

The bell rang. Susan didn't even try to end the class with a normal routine. She watched some students approach Linda with cautious words. One woman hugged her. Most of them, like Susan, gathered their belongings in silence and slowly left the room.

More than usual, Susan looked forward to her Friday afternoon conversation with her faculty mentor, Christine. She quickly sketched out the week for Christine, omitting none of the painful awkwardness of Linda's outburst.

"Holy smokes," breathed Christine. "What a tough class session! How did the students respond? Were they really blown away?"

"Yeah, I think they were. For many of the white students, I suspect they began to understand racism—perhaps for the first time. I expect this to be a big topic when I collect journals on Monday."

"So you think your students will write about this? That seems like a positive way to keep discussion going and get at some uncomfortable but important stuff. I hope they really confront the problems that Linda raises."

Susan bit her lip. "You're saying exactly what I've said to myself. Yet I'm still wondering where to go with this. I ask myself: who's learning, and at whose expense? When I think about it, I've been asking for trouble with these assignments. What happens when the descendants of slaves—or slave-owners—decide to speak up? What about the Jews who hold the Exodus story at the center of their faith? Can I really work on these issues in a responsible way? Who do I think I am?"

Christine examined her fingernails. Neither woman spoke for a long time.

# Dissin' The Prof

*by Susan J. Huber*
University of St. Thomas

## ABSTRACT

Diversity as a value in higher education brings with it some tricky problems. In this case, a model professor is confronted by a powerful, ambitious African-American woman who expects university standards to accommodate her life circumstances. Communication is complicated by the student's open disrespect for the professor and the professor's alleged racist attitude.

## POSSIBLE DISCUSSION QUESTIONS

1. As you read this case, do you find yourself remembering students like Pamela Fox and professors like Joanna Corbin? What is your experience with such folks?

2. This case catalogues accumulated irritation for both parties. How many ways does Pamela annoy Joanna? How many ways does Joanna annoy Pamela? Could either of them have diverted the course of this disastrous exchange?

3. What advice do you have for the administration of City College? Should the dean forward a discrimination complaint against Joanna? Should the Education Department admit Pamela as a major? Should either Joanna or Pamela be disciplined? If so, how? If not, why not?

4. As more nontraditional students enter higher education classrooms, what kind of training would help prepare faculty and students to encounter each other productively?

# Dissin' The Prof

Dr. Joanna Corbin, a seasoned professor in the Education Department, was ten minutes into an interactive lecture with her class of prospective education majors when Pamela Fox arrived and curtly interrupted her. "Dr. Corbin, will I be penalized for not handing in the assignment that's due today?" Pamela was referring to an assignment in the syllabus that requested students to attend a professional presentation related to teacher education and write a critique of it. She added she couldn't attend any of the presentations because she couldn't get a baby-sitter. Joanna, slightly taken aback by the timing of Pamela's question and the impertinent tone of it, responded sarcastically, "Pamela, if you don't hand in the assignment today, you obviously won't receive full credit." She immediately regretted the demeaning tone of voice she used to respond to Pamela, but justified it by thinking about Pamela's irksome pattern of coming late to class and then interrupting her to request information covered at the beginning of the hour.

Joanna, recently appointed Department Chair, was widely regarded as an excellent teacher. Students were routinely disappointed when her classes closed early each semester. They knew she would spend extra hours working with any student who needed help simply because she cared about teaching and about the students she taught. Nevertheless, she upheld high academic and performance standards and expected students to attend class, to exhibit eagerness for learning about the teaching profession, and to complete required course work as assigned. Each week as speakers came to campus, Joanna reminded her class of this assignment. Students knew they had several options for attending daytime or evening presentations. Joanna purposely built these options into the assignment because of the number of nontraditional-aged students in the class. She wondered why Pamela hadn't come to her privately to discuss any assignment accommodations she might need.

Pamela Fox was a strikingly lovely, statuesque, African-American woman whose eyes flashed with an intensity not easily forgotten. Joanna met her prior to the start of fall semester and remembered Pamela's telling her how interested she was in becoming a teacher. She had been a parent volunteer in her daughter's classroom and really enjoyed working with children. She was recently divorced and anxious about finding a career to provide an adequate income for her daughter and herself. At that first advising meeting, Pamela expressed concern about her 2.5 GPA, knowing she needed a 2.75 to be admitted to the Education Department. Pamela was a transfer student who appeared bright, articulate, and eager to move on with her life and her career.

As Joanna attempted to transition into cooperative group work, she noted that Pamela seemed visibly agitated. When the groups had finished their discussions, Joanna asked them to get ready for a critical incident check based on the work they had just completed. Pamela blurted out, "I won't be able to answer any of the questions. This stuff goes back to last week, and I wasn't here when you covered it." Joanna said more firmly than necessary, "I'm sorry, but we are having a check point. The information you missed from last week's class is in the text." Three other students who were also absent last week passed knowing looks from one to another.

Critical incident check points were accepted practice in this class. Joanna periodically provided students with a thought-provoking question, a case study, or an incident related to the topic under discussion. The "check" required students to reflect in writing for five minutes and then turn their paper in. Joanna explained to the students that these check points helped them evaluate their progress in class and helped her monitor her teaching.

Pamela appeared to be very angry. She turned her chair sideways to look out the windows; she drummed her fingers on her desk; she smoothed her check sheet and folded it into a perfect fan shape. Then she walked out of the class, excusing herself several times as her backpack swung into students seated in the back row. Joanna breathed a silent, "Thank goodness!" However, Pamela returned after a few minutes and chose a seat near the door. She glared at Joanna for the remainder of the class. When class ended, Joanna sensed that students were overly eager to leave.

Pamela eased toward the front of the room and motioned for people to keep moving. "I want to talk to you," she hissed at Joanna. "I'm not taking this anymore. I'm not going to be treated this way. This is the third time you've snipped me off, and you have no right. You're disrespectful, and I'm done with this. I've got an A in this class and I'm keeping it. Do you hear me?"

Joanna responded, "You had an A at midterm, Pamela. You will keep it if you earn it." Joanna and everyone ringing the door in the hallway heard Pamela shout, "What kind of a teacher are you, anyway? You're unfit to teach. You're supposed to be a role model and instead you're an insensitive bitch." Joanna, visibly shaken and embarrassed at the audience this outburst had attracted, asked Pamela to come to her office, hoping the movement might calm her down. Pamela held her tongue as they walked in silence down the hallway. As Joanna unlocked her office door, Pamela began the harangue again.

Pamela seemed to enjoy Joanna's discomfort. With eyes flashing, she leveled the charge: "You're racist. That's what I think you are! You're prejudiced! I'm the only African-American student in your class, and you're trying to prevent me from making it into the Department. I'm going to complain to the Dean and the President and anybody else I choose. I'm going to tell them you are a racist." Joanna was angered at Pamela's behavior and incensed at the litany of accusations being hurled at her.

Breathing deeply Joanna interrupted Pamela, and asked her if she thought she could deal with her anger in a more respectful manner. As Pamela sat down, Joanna smiled slightly, hoping they would now come to terms. Joanna went on, "I think two adult women should be able to discuss this problem with civility, don't you?".

Pamela, carefully forming each syllable, said, "Dr. Corbin, I don't have to respect you. I pay your salary." At that point Joanna chose to disengage from any further conversation. Pamela wanted argumentation. When she received silence, she went on to cite the three incidents that provoked her. The first week of the semester, on a day Pamela was absent from class, Joanna passed around a sign-up sheet for a partner assignment. By the time Pamela came to Joanna's office to sign up, all the students had chosen their partners. Joanna had told her she could choose to work in a threesome, work with a student in her other section, or work by herself. "These weren't suitable options," Pamela insisted. "They were discriminatory."

Pamela went on with number two. "When I called you at home about our research assignment, I politely said I was sorry to bother you on a Sunday morning, and you just said, 'That's O.K.' You sounded as if you didn't care about my question. Maybe you wanted me to fail.

"Today in class you said I had to hand in the assignment to receive credit when I told you I had no child care. I'm 28 years old. I'm not like those other students. You don't tell me like I'm sixteen that I gotta do something."

Pamela grabbed her backpack and stood tall in the doorway of the office. "Everybody thinks you're such a good teacher. Well, they're wrong. Why don't you just go back to the suburbs where you belong? I'm going to complain about discriminatory treatment in this Department. I'm going to a higher authority than you. You have no business being Department Chair anyway. I'm going to the Dean."

Joanna knew better than to respond, but anger won out. In her most authoritarian voice, she said, "Pamela, I encourage you to go speak to whomever you wish. I hope you are more civil to them than you have been to me. If your intention was to hurt my feelings, you have succeeded, but I will remain Chair of this Department."

Slumped in her chair, heart thumping from the confrontation, Joanna tried to critically assess the situation. What provoked Pamela to call her a racist? That label really stung. She felt Pamela's comments were not only hurtful and accusatory, but blatantly false. No student had ever challenged her in that manner or accused her of being racially prejudiced. She thought about the recommendation she wrote for Pamela to help her secure a scholarship for women of color. She remembered the phone calls she made to create a special educational field experience for her to suit her child-care schedule. She also thought about Pamela's habitual tardiness. She hadn't ever asked her if something prevented her from getting to class on time. Child care or a part-time job could be complicating the issue. In actuality, she hadn't spent much time getting to know Pamela. Pamela never lingered after class to talk like so many of the others.

Once again, Joanna recalled her initial meeting with Pamela. Don Helgersen, the outgoing Department Chair, introduced the two of them in his typical manner and said, "Let's see what you can do for our new transfer student, Pamela." Joanna wondered if Don had told Pamela her grades would be no problem for admittance into the Department. Don seemed to make a habit of telling all students that grades would be no problem. He expected the faculty advisors to straighten out any GPA issues, and, if a student really protested, he always found a way to make things work out favorably for the student. After all, he was the Department Chair, and he could override a faculty recommendation stipulating no admittance due to low GPA with a conditional admittance. Don believed in giving everyone a chance, and besides that he hated conflict. Savvy students knew exactly how to work this system.

Joanna Corbin, as new Chair of the Department, brought her reputation with her. She would be fair to all students trying to gain admittance to the Department, but she didn't cut deals. Students who didn't meet the criteria for admittance would have to bring up their GPA to meet departmental standards prior to being accepted into the department. This new way of doing business was making more than a few students anxious. For some it might mean spending an extra semester to bring up their GPA. Pamela Fox did not meet the required standard. She was clearly interested in earning a teaching license ASAP and getting on with her career. Joanna Corbin looked to be the potential stumbling block.

Charges of racism were never treated lightly at City College. The thought of Pamela citing her for discriminatory treatment angered Joanna. The Grievance Committee's investigation, regardless of the outcome, would certainly mar her unblemished reputation. She wondered if Pamela would be bold enough to return to class. What if she refused to admit her? The pending departmental admission interviews presented a more troubling problem. Pamela's GPA should disqualify her from admittance to the Department. Joanna, as Department Chair, could recommend conditional admission for Pamela. What action should Joanna Corbin take?

# Bibliography

## Books

Anson, Chris M., Joan Graham, David A. Jolliffe, Carolyn Smith, and Nancy Shapiro. *Scenarios for Teaching Writing: Contexts for Discussion and Reflective Practice.* Urbana, Ill: National Council of Teachers of English/Alliance for Undergraduate Education, 1993.

Barnes, L., C. Christensen, and A. Hansen, *Teaching and The Case Method.* (3rd edition). Boston: Harvard University Press, 1994.

Christensen, C. Roland, David A. Garvin, and Ann Sweet, eds. *Education for Judgment: The Artistry of Discussion Leadership.* Boston: Harvard Business School Press, 1991.

Christensen, C. Roland with Abby J. Hansen. *Teaching and the Case Method.* Boston: Harvard Business School Publishing Division, 1986.

Christensen, C. Roland with Abby J. Hansen and James F. Moore. *Teaching and the Case Method: Instructor's Guide.* Boston: Harvard Business School Publishing Division, 1986.

Cross, K. Patricia and Mimi Harris Steadman. *Implementing the Scholarship of Teaching.* San Francisco: Jossey-Bass, 1996.

Higgerson, Mary Lou and Susan S. Rehwaldt. *Complexities of Higher Education Administration: Case Studies & Issues.* Bolton, Mass.: Anker Publishing Company, Inc., 1993.

Hutchings, Patricia. *Using Cases to Improve College Teaching: A Guide to More Reflective Practice.* Washington, D.C.: American Association for Higher Education, 1993.

Jones, Thomas B. and Chet Myers. *Promoting Active Learning: Strategies for the College Classroom.* San Francisco: Jossey-Bass, 1993.

Lang, Cynthia. *Case Method Teaching in the Community College.* Newton, Mass: Educational Development Center, 1986.

McAninch, Amy Raths. *Teacher Thinking and the Case Method: Theory and Future Practice.* New York: Teachers College Press, 1993.

Merseth, Katherine. *The Case for Cases in Teacher Education.* Washington, D.C.: American Association for Higher Education, 1991.

Schön, Donald A. *The Reflective Practitioner: How Professionals Think in Action.* New York: Basic Books, 1983.

Schön, Donald A., ed. *The Reflective Turn: Case Studies in and on Educational Practice.* New York: Teachers College Press, 1991.

Shulman, Judith H., ed. *Case Methods in Teacher Education.* New York: Teachers College Press, 1992.

Silverman, Rita, William M. Welty and Sally Lyon. *Case Studies for Teacher Problem Solving.* New York: McGraw-Hill, 1992.

———. *Case Studies for Teacher Problem Solving: Instructor's Manual.* New York: McGraw-Hill, 1992.

Smith, Barbara Leigh. *Washington Center Casebook on Collaborative Teaching and Learning.* Olympia, Washington: The Washington Center for Improving the Quality of Undergraduate Education at The Evergreen State College, 1993.

Tedesco, P.H. *Teaching with Case Studies.* Boston: Public Information Center, Federal Reserve Bank of Boston, 1974.

Wasserman, Selma. *Getting Down to Cases: Learning to Teach with Case Studies.* New York: Teachers College Press, 1993.

———. *Introduction to Case Method Teaching: A Guide to the Galaxy.* New York: Teachers College Press, 1994.

Wasley, Patricia A. *Stirring the Chalkdust: Tales of Teachers Changing Classroom Practice.* New York: Teachers College Press, 1994.

## Articles

Anson, Chris M., David A. Jolliffe, and Nancy Shapiro. "Toward Reflective Practice: Using Scenarios in TA and Faculty Development." *WPA: Writing Program Administration,* Fall 1993.

Barnett, Carne. "Building a Case-Based Curriculum to Enhance the Pedagogical Content Knowledge of Mathematics Teachers." *Journal of Teacher Education* (September/October 1991).

———. "The Use of Cases in Management Education." Available as a reprint from HBS Publishing Division, Harvard Business School, Boston, Case #376-240 (1976).

Barrows, Howard S. "Problem-Based Learning in Medicine and Beyond: A Brief Overview." *New Directions for Teaching and Learning,* 68 (Winter 1996): 3-12.

Bruss, Kristine S. "Using the Case Method to Promote Freshman Seminar Goals." *Journal of College Student Development.* 37 (Jan.-Feb. 1996): 98-100.

Elmore, Richard. "How We Teach is What We Teach." *AAHE Bulletin,* 41 (1989).

Fineberg, Warren and Lawrence Ingvarson. "Developing and Using Cases of Pedagogical Content Knowledge in the Professional Development of Science Teachers." Paper presented at the 1992 American Educational Research Association Annual Meeting, San Francisco.

Frederick, Peter. "The Dreaded Discussion: Ten Ways to Start." *Improving College and University Teaching.* 29 (1981).

Harrington, Helen L. "Fostering Reasoned Decision: Case-Based Pedagogy and the Professional Development of Teachers." *Teaching and Teacher Education.* 11/3 (1995): 203-14.

Smith, Karl. "Cooperative Learning: Effective Teamwork for Engineering Classrooms." *ASEE Electrical Engineering Division Newsletter.* IEEE Education Society, March 1995.

Smith, Ronald A. and Fred Schwartz. "Improving Teaching by Reflecting on Practice." *To Improve the Academy: Resources for Student, Faculty, and Institutional Development.* 7 (1988).

Welty, William M. "Discussion Method Teaching: How to Make It Work." *Change* (July/August, 1989).

Wilkerson, LuAnn and John Boehrer. "Using Cases about Teaching for Faculty Development." *To Improve the Academy: Resources for Faculty, Instructional, and Organizational Development.* 11 (1992).

## Internet Sites

Duin, Ann Hill and Steve R. Simmons. *Decision Cases for Writing Across the Curriculum.* Minneapolis: Center for the Interdisciplinary Study of Writing, University of Minnesota. www.cisw.cla.umn.edu/Admin/Research/Cross/Duin.html.

Ethics Center for Engineering & Science. *Engineering Ethics Cases Section.* Cleveland: Ethics Center for Engineering & Science, Case Western Reserve University. www.cwru.edu/affil/wwwethics/engcases.html.

Hollander, Scott and Nancy Schiller. *Case Studies in Science.* Buffalo: State University of New York. ublib.buffalo.edu/libraries/projects/cases/case.html.

Program for Decision Cases. *The Clearinghouse for Decision Case Education: Agriculture, Food, Natural Resources and the Environment.* St. Paul: University of Minnesota. www.decisioncase.edu.